100 Ideas for Primary Teachers:

Literacy

Other titles in the 100 Ideas for Primary Teachers series:

100 Ideas for Primary Teachers:

Literacy

Rob Smith and Katherine Simpson

BLOOMSBURY
LONDON • OXFORD • NEW YORK • NEW DELHI • SYDNEY

Bloomsbury Education
An imprint of Bloomsbury Publishing Plc

50 Bedford Square	1385 Broadway
London	New York
WC1B 3DP	NY 10018
UK	USA

www.bloomsbury.com

BLOOMSBURY and the Diana logo are trademarks of
Bloomsbury Publishing Plc

First published in Great Britain 2018

ISBN:
PB: 9781472948861
ePub: 9781472948878
ePDF: 9781472948854

2 4 6 8 10 9 7 5 3 1

Typeset by Newgen Knowledge Works Pvt. Ltd., Chennai, India
Printed and bound by CPI Group (UK) Ltd, Croydon, CR0 4YY

This book is produced using paper that is made from wood grown in
managed, sustainable forests. It is natural, renewable and recyclable.
The logging and manufacturing processes conform to
the environmental regulations of the country of origin.

To find out more about our authors and books visit www.bloomsbury.com.
Here you will find extracts, author interviews, details of forthcoming events
and the option to sign up for our newsletters.

Contents

Acknowledgements

Firstly, we are eternally grateful to our wonderful families for the love, support and belief in all we do. Your confidence in our abilities and your wonderful optimism about our endeavours keep us motivated to do more.

Rod and Liz – you've given us the opportunity to follow our dreams and for that we are eternally thankful.

Paul and Elaine – those uni fees were worth it! But joking aside, you've encouraged and supported us through some big decisions and we thank you from the bottom of our hearts.

We would like to thank the tens of thousands of you who have chosen to follow us, shared your ideas, used our ideas, reached out to us when you've needed support and offered us help when we've needed it. You are our teaching army and we feel privileged to be amongst your ranks.

Thank you also to Joe and his amazing team at The Hungry Duck for our outstanding work breakfasts and to Adrian and his fabulous team at Grind and Tamp for keeping us caffeinated and supplying us with some fantastic 'work' music.

A special thanks needs to be made to the fabulous children who we have had the pleasure of teaching over our many years in the classroom. You are the reason we wanted to write this book and the reason we both love English so much.

This book is dedicated to two little boys: Noah and Monty. You are the reason we smile every day. Thank you for being such superstars and for loving books even more than we do.

Introduction

Let us begin, perhaps a little oddly, by telling you what this book is not: it is *not* our way of telling you how English should be taught. It is *not* a one-size-fits-all approach, and neither is it designed to be a quick fix for English. We do *not* know the children in your class, or their abilities, their likes, their dislikes, what motivates them or what keeps them hooked. It is *not* intended to replace your planning; nor will it tidy your classroom at the end of the day — though it would be rather marvellous if it could!

However, it *is* a book of tried-and-tested ideas which have had a significant impact upon our English teaching and the children we have taught. It *is* a book of suggestions for how you might approach certain elements of the teaching of English. It *is* a book full of ideas designed to be adapted and modified. In fact, it is full of ideas which have been used and tweaked and improved and reimagined many times over, and we expect you will want to do the same.

We have categorised the book into a number of sections for ease of use. The ideas cover themes such as word and spelling games, activities to support the teaching of reading, ideas for poetry, using film and images in the classroom and the teaching of grammar. We focus upon the teaching of writing and make suggestions for a wide range of lessons — from using social media updates as a hook into writing, to how to write an epic ending.

Some of the ideas are designed to be used perhaps once a year as 'one-offs' and certainly not repeated within the same class; many of the ideas are designed to be used more regularly and could fit in within any unit of English, or even be used daily. Several of the pages offer up a host of ideas around one theme and others stick to a more procedural approach to teaching one specific activity. All of the ideas are intended to be simple to follow and easy to replicate.

Ultimately, we want you to use the book to do more than just dot the i's and cross the t's. We want you to use it to add sparkle and smiles to your lessons. We want the grammar groan (the exhaling sound a teacher makes when faced with teaching semicolons) to be a thing of the past. We want you to feel confident, inspired and enthusiastic about your English lessons, because, let's face it, when you feel that way, so do the children.

How to use this book

This book includes quick, easy, practical ideas and guidance for you to dip in and out of, to help you plan and carry out literacy activities for the children in your care.

Each idea includes:

- a catchy title, easy to refer to and share with your colleagues
- a quote from a practitioner, parent or child, describing their experience that has led to the idea
- a summary of the idea in bold, making it easy to flick through the book and identify an idea you want to use at a glance
- a step-by-step guide to implementing the idea.

Each idea also includes one or more of the following:

Teaching tip	Taking it further	Bonus idea ★
Practical tips and advice for how and how not to run the activity or put the idea into practice.	Ideas and advice for how to extend the idea or develop it further.	**There are 19 bonus ideas in this book that are extra exciting, extra original and extra interesting.**

Share how you use these ideas and find out what other practitioners have done using **#100ideas**.

Online resources for this book can be found at www.bloomsbury.com/100-ideas-primary-literacy.

Word power

Part 1

Word of the week/day

"Using the word of the day has really helped to broaden the children's vocabulary."

Using word of the week/day is a great way to introduce new vocabulary and build up a bank of words for children to use.

Begin by giving the word of the week/day to the children in a context. This could be underlined in a piece of text or in a sentence. Can the children use the context to understand what the word means? Offer three suggestions and allow the children to decide which they think is correct. Discuss the word class of the word. Does it fall into more than one?

Nestling

The nestling was not old enough to leave the nest.

Nestling himself into the hay, he drifted off into an uneasy sleep.

Activities to use alongside word of the week/day

- Synonym and antonym hunt – find as many as possible.
- Ten-sentence challenge – can the children write the word in 10 different sentences?
- Word position – can the children write the word in different positions in the sentence?
- Hidden words – can the children find any other words hidden within the word?
- Dictionary – ask the children to find the words which come either side of the word in the dictionary.
- Spelling it – add the word to the children's spelling list for the week.
- Rhyming words – how many words can the children think of to rhyme with it?
- Vowel mirror – find the vowels in the word, then see how many other words have the same combination of vowels in that position and order, e.g. NESTLING – PERCHING.

Improvement stations

"I teach the improvement stations by explaining that a station is somewhere you stop and decide what to do next on your journey."

With a little advanced preparation, the idea of improvement stations can be adapted to suit a wide range of lessons, ages and abilities.

You need to prepare each table as a different station to be used to improve the children's work. This also needs to be appropriate for the task. In this example, we imagine the children are creating setting descriptions.

A Year 5/6 class, with six tables, could be arranged in the following way:

Table 1 – Verbs
Table 2 – Prepositional starters
Table 3 – Adverbs
Table 4 – Senses
Table 5 – Adjectives
Table 6 – Figurative language.

At the beginning of the lesson, give out several simple sentences, or ask the children to create some themselves. Ensure there are whiteboards and pens available for the children to play with the vocabulary. On each table, have a 'Why not try . . . ?' idea so that the children are encouraged to do more than simply insert a word, e.g. 'try opening with the verb' or 'try placing three verbs as an opener'. They should then be given a few minutes on each table to complete a number of different tasks depending upon the station they are at. Some teachers like to provide laminated cards with vocabulary and phrases on, though this can be time-consuming. It is just as useful to provide word bank sheets, sentence starters and tablets with vocabulary examples, etc.

Teaching tip

Ask the children to stop after each station and decide upon their favourite change. At the end of the process, ask the children to comment on what they found to be successful. Share ideas and ask the children to swap an idea with their neighbour and try it out themselves.

Bonus idea ★

This could also be used as an editing task when the children have already created a paragraph of double-spaced writing.

Spelling games

"We absolutely love playing stickman showdown because we work as a team to try and keep our stickman alive!"

Spelling games can help to consolidate rules, recognise patterns, identify misconceptions, problem solve and review learning — and they are fun!

Stickman showdown

Ask two team captains to each draw a stickman on the board. They should use the same number of body parts. Stand the two teams in two rows. As you call the first word, the children step forwards to spell it on a whiteboard. If it is correct, they keep the stickman. If either team get it wrong, then the opposing team is allowed to rub out one of the stickman's lines. The team who loses is the first team to lose their stickman.

Word ladders

Provide the children with a starter word of four letters, e.g. *want*. Next, the children must write the word again underneath, changing one letter to make it into a new word — without repetitions. How many new words can they form by only changing one letter? Could they try five letters? Could they try to get from one word to another? Here's an example:

want → *went* → *tent* → *tint*

Splat-a-word

Prepare in advance a selection of word cards which fit the criteria you would like to test. Also provide some that do not. Clear an area on the carpet and put the words face up. Provide two children with something to 'splat' with — a fly swatter is useful. The rest of the children need to count the players' scores. Set a timer for a minute and call out the criteria for the children to meet, e.g. 'Splat the long vowel sound *a*'. The players 'splat' the corresponding words.

Choosing appropriate language for effect

"It makes the reader want to read on."

Word banks have their uses, as do the enduring vocabulary pyramids which decorate classroom walls around the country. It is essential, however, when using these word banks, that pupils understand WHY it is that they are choosing a particular word or phrase and also the effect that it will have on their audience.

It is important to share examples to illustrate the difference a carefully-chosen word can make in a sentence and also the problem that exaggerating language can have on meaning. For example, when substituting the word 'sad' for a more powerful synonym, a child looking in a thesaurus may get this list:

bereaved, blue, cheerless, dejected, despairing, despondent, disconsolate, distressed, doleful, down, downcast, down in the dumps, forlorn, gloomy, glum, grief-stricken, grieved, heartsick, hurting, languishing, low, lugubrious, morbid, morose, pensive, woebegone.

(Taken from www.thesaurus.com)

If a child were to choose one of these words to substitute 'sad' in a sentence, then the meaning may alter considerably.

Sarah was grief-stricken because she couldn't attend the school disco.

Sarah left her father's graveside feeling down in the dumps about her loss.

Neither of these choices would be appropriate for the context. It is at this point that direct teaching of vocabulary and meaning is important. Spend time looking at synonyms and discussing the nuances between words.

Teaching tip

Do not give out word banks and thesauruses without modelling use and discussing key words and phrases.

Teach vocabulary and be explicit

"'Who can think of a better way to describe how dark the forest is?' asks the teacher expectantly. 'Very dark!' an eager respondent blurts out."

Thesauruses rely upon knowing the subtle differences between the words on offer. It is much quicker and more powerful to give the children a number of interesting options which they can use in their writing and apply in later sessions too.

Taking it further

If we share 30 words per week in this way, every week over the school year, then that will be over 1,000 new words children learn every year to accurately incorporate into their writing.

It is important that we introduce words and phrases in context. When writing ghost stories, for example, introduce a selection of powerful words that could be used within that genre. Produce the list prior to the lesson and display it prominently. If studying a model text, select vocabulary from the text. When using a film or image, choose words which would be useful when describing what they can see. The book *Descriptosaurus* by Alison Wilcox features vocabulary and phrases which are categorised and ready to use. Over the course of a unit of work, the children and the teacher can add to their list as they find examples through reading and discussion.

The key to children using the vocabulary effectively is to understand *why* it has been used by the author. For example, in the description of a forest below, the author chooses words (in bold) which build up an image of death in the reader's mind.

*'The forest was cloaked in **darkness**: the trees **shrouded** in mist. From the **black skeletal** branches, **dead** leaves fell drifting down in a twisted danse **macabre**.'*

They could have simply written, *'It was a deathly forest'*. However, the carefully chosen language allows the reader to develop this image for themselves.

Vocabulary stations

"The limits of my language mean the limits of my world." – Ludwig Wittgenstein

With the flourish of a pen, authors can create worlds which come alive and characters who leave an indelible mark on our hearts. All children can produce creative writing; however, some can be held back due to a deficit of vocabulary. There are a number of ways in which vocabulary can be improved: reading is key, but good teacher models, language discussions and the language of their peers all play a part.

Within every class, there is a range of vocabulary levels. It is important that high-quality vocabulary be shared and utilised by all. As teachers, we often encourage pupils to steal, pinch or 'magpie' great examples of vocabulary from authors and our models, but we also need to encourage them to borrow it from their peers.

'Vocabulary stations' are an effective and inclusive way of doing this. In this activity, 'stations' are placed around the room for the children to add their vocabulary suggestions on using sticky notes.

Beforehand, decide on the writing outcome; this activity often works best for descriptive writing. Decide upon the main components for the subject of the description, e.g. components for a landscape could be:

- Trees
- Sky
- Lake
- Path
- Clouds
- Sun.

All that is needed for each station is a simple label stuck to a space in the classroom. The children then write a descriptive word, phrase or sentence for each of the stations on a sticky note, add it to the appropriate vocabulary station and repeat. Children can choose to add many descriptions to one station or add descriptions to each one. The children then need to read the suggestions at each station.

Taking it further

Model the gathering of ideas from each station to create a text. The children should then copy this process in order to create their own descriptive passage of writing.

Word games

"I love going through my teacher's rubbish bin to look for the words that shouldn't have been thrown away!"

Children love to learn through play. Have a bank of word games which can be pulled out at any convenient moment, and use them to consolidate knowledge or introduce new learning.

Connect 4

This is a really simple 'sight word' game. You will need a Connect 4 game or something similar. Create a set of flash cards with vocabulary to learn. The child must correctly read the word before they can place their corresponding counter into the Connect 4 grid. Play until one child creates a row.

Jenga

Using an old game of Jenga, stick a small strip of masking tape onto each block so that you can write on them. Now add new vocabulary/ spelling words/technical vocabulary to the blocks. The children play the game of Jenga as usual, though when they successfully draw the Jenga block, they must put the vocabulary into a sentence or explain the meaning of the word. They are only allowed to place the block on the top of the tower if they are successful. If they complete both steps, the team wins a point. If they knock the tower over, the team loses five points.

Bin it or keep it

Provide the children with a waste paper bin full of screwed up paper with words, phrases or sentences on – this needs to suit the task. Explain that they need to work their way through each piece of paper to separate them into piles, e.g. 'Bin the nouns and keep the adjectives', 'Bin the nonsense words and keep the real words' or 'Bin the poor punctuation and keep the accurately-punctuated sentences'.

Boggle

Based upon the game of the same name, provide the children with a nine-letter word, scrambled in a 3 x 3 grid. Allocate a points system to words of different lengths, e.g. 'A three-letter word scores one point and a four-letter word scores two points'. The children should be given a short amount of time to look for words hidden within the nine-letter word. This could be extended by asking children to only use letters which are directly adjacent to each other.

Scrabble tile

Provide the children with an image that shows Scrabble tiles with their values. Then give them a list of criteria to meet. Can they find a word with a total of 21? Can they find a word which scores fewer points than there are letters in the word? Or, show the children a selection of Scrabble tiles and challenge the children to make the highest-scoring word and the lowest-scoring three-letter word.

Battleships

Using Battleships-style grids, the children need to write words of differing lengths onto the board. Their opponent should not see their board. Words can intersect one another when they share a letter. The children should then play Battleships. If the guesser gets a 'hit', then the other player must tell them the letter they've landed on. They need to find more letters until they can guess the word. They still need to spell it correctly to win the points though!

> **Bonus idea** ★
>
> Using one dictionary, and making sure the children cannot see the answers, select two words which are fairly close together in the dictionary. Write them on the board for the children to see, e.g. 'plumber' and 'poach'. Can the children identify a word which is found between them?

Pre-teaching technical vocabulary

"Few activities are as delightful as learning new vocabulary." — Ludwig Wittgenstein

There are many times when using specific language makes an author sound like an expert on the topic they are writing about. It is important that children are exposed to this kind of language in order to be able to replicate it in their own writing. It is often prudent to expose the children to the technical and specific language before they encounter it in their own reading.

Whilst reading the text prior to teaching, you should select a number of words which may need additional clarification. It is these words that you will pre-teach before the children read the text. Choose approximately 3–5 words; don't overwhelm the children with the language as this could overshadow the reading process.

1 Read the new word with the children and support any pronunciation difficulties.
2 Ask the children what they think the word might mean. There could be some clues in the spelling. For example, *-ology* may direct the children towards scientific words.
3 Share a simplified definition that the children will understand and discuss when and how the word could be used, e.g. *inconsolable* can be defined as very sad, but it is not always appropriate to use the term to describe sadness.
4 Ask the children to put the new word into a sentence. This can be done orally or on whiteboards. Check their sentence for understanding and share examples of effective use.
5 When reading, highlight the word and discuss the meaning again in context.

Vocabulary bingo

"I love playing bingo in class because, even though I am learning, it's a fun game and it gets me excited when I can shout 'BINGO!'"

Vocabulary bingo can be a useful activity for teaching new spellings, learning new vocabulary, checking the children's understanding of word classes and keeping the children engaged. There are several different ways to play, so here are just a few.

Method 1
Give out blank bingo cards on a 4 x 4 grid. Give the children a list of words to choose from. This game works well when learning spellings or working with longer lists. The children need to select 16 words from the list and write them into their grid. Once the children have filled the grids, the caller begins to randomly call out the definitions of the words. Children locate the words and cross them off. First to fill a line wins bingo.

> **Teaching tip**
>
> Check out the Online Resources for this book for a printable bingo grid.

Method 2
Give out a page or pages from a book. Select a word class for the children to use – make sure there are plenty of whatever it is you choose. Give out a 4 x 4 grid for the children to add their words to. The children should work through the text and select 16 words of the corresponding word class you have asked for. Then play bingo as normal.

Method 3
Provide the children with a 4 x 4 grid. Have a pre-prepared list of adjectives. The children should select 16 of the adjectives to fill their grid. Next, randomly select words from the list, but instead of saying the word, give them an antonym. The children need to correctly identify their word and cross it off. First to fill a line wins.

> **Taking it further**
>
> With younger children, or children learning English as an additional language, use physical objects to place onto the grids to match with initial or final letter sounds.

Shake and roll vocabulary activities

"Nanny Ogg knew how to start spelling 'banana', but didn't know how you stopped." – Terry Pratchett, *Witches Abroad*

Many schools use word journals or vocabulary books to collect and record new words. They also add to these books any new words which they come across when reading. By using shake and roll activities, alongside new vocabulary, words are learned and retained with greater success.

Taking it further

It is useful to ensure children take word journals or vocabulary books to their new class each year, so that the process is ongoing and previously found words are not forgotten.

Using a die or random number generator app, children 'choose' which activity to work on in their vocabulary journal. This could be something that they do each morning with the word of the day (see Idea 1) or something they do during English or reading lessons when they come across a new or interesting word.

Select six activities – relevant to your class – and number them, e.g. 'when the number 1 is rolled, draw a quick sketch to illustrate the word'.

Other activities could include:

- List three synonyms
- Create a definition in your own words
- Think of some words with similar letter strings
- Find some words that rhyme
- Put the word into a sentence
- Classify the word – noun, adjective, verb, etc.
- Record some other forms of the word.

Choose a range from the list above in order to reinforce spelling and/or meaning, or add some of your own which are relevant to their class.

Teaching tip

To make the vocabulary more meaningful when looking up the words in their journal, children can add a definition or illustration in order to refresh their memory of the word's specific meaning.

Reading

Part 2

Be a book expert

"A reader lives a thousand lives before he dies. The man who never reads lives only one." – George R. R. Martin

The National Literacy Trust reported in 2014 that, 'Good reading habits formed at a young age meant individuals had better vocabulary later in life'. This is just one of the benefits of developing good reading habits.

For many children, the class teacher is the adult in their life who models good reading habits. Where this is the case, it is imperative that the teacher has the knowledge and experience of a wide range of books in order to recommend them to children. Once children begin to read the books, the teacher can further encourage the pupils by discussing their reading books with them. In our experience, when the class teacher is excited about a text, then the child becomes excited about it too. If you can say to a child, 'Have you got up to this bit yet?' or 'My favourite character is x – who's yours?', then you open up a dialogue which makes the child, and the reading that they are doing, feel valued.

Where to start?
- If you have a library, then start by reading those books. Place a sticker on the front or a bookmark inside which reads 'Teacher Recommended'.
- Start a small class lending library of books which you have read and recommend them to the children based on their interests.

Where to find the texts
- The Literacy Shed: Book of the Week
- Centre for Literacy in Primary English Core book list
- The Book Trust: 100 best books
- TES: 100 fiction books all children should read before leaving primary school.

Creating a reading-rich environment

"Our visitors always comment about the fact there are children reading everywhere!"

Within the classroom, children will often have access to reading books, whole-class reading books, class library books, boxes of topic-based books, guided reading books, tablets and laptops, magazines and newspapers, displays, games and much more. It is essential, however, that this reading does not stop as soon as they step out of the classroom door.

Books on the playground
Assign some children to take out some book boxes onto the playground during playtime. Ensure there is a range of books to encourage different readers, and create a reading area to sit in.

Books in the hall
At lunchtime, provide the children with book boxes on the tables. Encourage the children to enjoy reciprocal reading with children from other years.

Books in assembly
Host a weekly reading assembly. Have a weekly theme and ask some children to read a short section from their favourite books.

Books on the school website
Have an 'Our favourite reads' section on the school website. Children could blog about their favourite authors and have a book recommendation section.

Books in the library
It goes without saying that a school library contains books. However, are children allowed to take library books home? Are book activities run there? Is the library open at break and lunchtimes? Are the children young librarians?

> **Teaching tip**
>
> All staff could have a sign on their door saying, 'This week I am reading . . .' with a summary of a children's book.

> **Bonus idea** ★
>
> Books after school
> An after school book club is a lovely way to share a love of reading. Ensure there are enough copies to take home and encourage the children to respond to the text through art, drama, poetry, writing or display.

Guest readers

"As a child, nothing gave me more joy than to hear my head teacher's voice at the door as he came to announce he would be reading another *What-a-Mess* story to us."

Having a 'guest reader' in the classroom can be such a pleasurable experience for all involved. Guest readers can enthuse the children, help to forge links with the community and create incredibly memorable reading moments.

Guest readers in the classroom can be organised in different ways. One of the most successful methods I have seen is when the children are unaware of guest readers coming into their classroom. I remember, vividly, watching the children's mouths open in shock when the chair of governors (who was well known within the school community) walked into the classroom with a book, sat on the chair at the front, and began to read. There were a few nervous giggles, but after the initial shock, it was an absolute pleasure to watch. Guest readers could be selected from many different sources: parents, grandparents, governors, the head teacher, the catering staff, the crossing patrol attendant or the school nurse, to name just a few.

The surprise visit always has most impact. Several reading slots could be arranged and then, on different days, or at different times, guest readers could 'drop in' and read their favourite children's book. There is often a great deal of book talk after the reading when an unread or lesser-known book is chosen.

As part of some topics/units of work, it might be possible to have guest experts attend the school to read to different groups of children. Ask the children to prepare questions in advance if the topic is quite new to them.

Early discussions

"How do you know that the character is feeling that way?"

Discussing 'why' with pupils is a key part of the comprehension process. The ability to comprehend what is being read is the measure of a reader's ability; therefore, the ability to explain their understanding, succinctly, is essential.

These discussions are sometimes started too late; an emphasis on decoding and retrieval skills in young children means that they can find it difficult to express and then explain their opinions. Children need to rehearse giving their opinion and backing it up with evidence from the text.

The process should start with oral rehearsal, through informal discussion with the adults they read with. As well as closed response questions, children should be asked their opinions and encouraged to explain how or why they formed them. For example, when asked about the characters' feelings, if the child's response is limited, the adult needs to question further and ask, 'How do you know that?'. Children should always be able to respond with 'I know . . . because of . . .'.

This process should start as soon as children begin to read. Teachers of young children and non-readers can start the discussions during those times when they are sharing books together.

Once they have orally rehearsed the process, this can then be formalised through written responses using scaffolds such as 'Point, Evidence, Explain' (P.E.E.).

> **Teaching tip**
>
> If there are a number of different adults reading with children, it may be prudent to provide a set of question stems to support consistency of questioning.

> **Bonus idea** ★
>
> An alternative to P.E.E. is 'A.P.E.' – Answer, Point, Explain. You can read more about this on Mrs P's Blog (www.mrspteach.com).

Scaffolding questioning

"When I discuss reading with my teacher, I find out things that I hadn't even noticed."

There may be a guided reading carousel, whole-class guided reading, reciprocal reading, and one-to-one reading with an adult all happening in the same setting. It is important to develop a consistent approach to questioning across all of these reading scenarios.

Teaching tip

Try applying VIPERS questions to films and images to reinforce their use.

Schools can create their own generic question stems based on the key comprehension skills. We have decided on these key areas: **V**ocabulary, **I**nference, **P**rediction, **E**xplanation, **R**etrieval, **S**ummarise and sequence.

As you can see, these skills present us with a mnemonic (VIPERS) which will make them easy to remember for both staff and children.

V – Vocabulary questions look at the meaning of the words in context.

I – Inference questions ask the children to explain their thoughts on the text, based on clues.

P – Children are asked to predict what they think will happen next and how characters will react, based on what they have read.

E – Younger children may explain their preferences and opinions about the text, whereas older children may explain why they think the text has been organised in a certain way, why the author has chosen to use particular language, and whether they have found any patterns in the text.

R – Here the teacher asks the children to retrieve key information from a range of texts.

S – Sequence the events in the text. Summarise the key events, characters or feelings across a section, or the whole text.

CSI – crime scene inference

"Providing the children with clues to read requires them to use their inference and deduction skills."

One method of teaching inference and deduction to children, which we have found to be extremely successful, is the use of an imaginary crime scene. Children love the idea of solving a crime; and the idea of reading a detective's notes is something of a thrill for the children.

This activity does take some preparation. During preparation time, decide upon one or two perpetrators and the crime they will have committed – be very careful when selecting the crime as this could be a potentially frightening activity. We have used a robbery at the Museum of Cairo, a theft of an item of jewellery from a stately home, and an attempt to steal cars from a celebrity. Decide upon how this person/people perpetrated the crime – this shouldn't be too complex for the children to be able to solve. Next, produce a set of crime clues and police notes for the children to read. Ensure that there are some 'red herrings' for the children to have to deliberate over.

Begin with a presentation of 'suspects' for the children to select from. Provide them with the clues and detective's crime notes to help narrow down the suspects, e.g. a set of car keys was dropped at the crime scene (provide information that somebody doesn't drive, so that they can be ruled out). The children should work their way through the clues and notes as a group and decide who can be ruled out and why. Always provide the children with a format for recording their notes. Every ten minutes, ask the groups to share one of the clues they have used to discount a suspect and explain why. Give the children around half an hour to 45 minutes to solve the crime.

Teaching tip

Use the lesson to develop a newspaper article about the crime.

Taking it further

For the groups who think they may have solved the crime, ask the children to prepare a group presentation to explain their thinking.

Book ticking challenge

"The readers embraced the need to read more widely as they wanted to tick off their list."

This is an idea that came to us in the pub (as all the best ones do!). Beer ticking is a social phenomenon that sees people creating lists of beers, on a theme. They then challenge others to see how many they can tick off. Here we apply the same idea to books.

Teaching tip

Use this activity for reading and discussing the books. Children begin to tell each other, 'I read one that was written in the first person and it is x'. Award points for activities.

This is a great idea for competitive readers who wouldn't be choosing books based on their own preferences, but on the criteria set out on the book tick list. This would then expose those children with narrow preferences to a whole range of texts.

Here is an example fiction book ticking challenge with 32 books to collect.

Can you tell me a book that . . .

. . . has a girl in the leading role?
. . . has a football team in it?
. . . has a character who is a ghost?
. . . is about Christmas?
. . . is not set on Earth?
. . . made you laugh at some point?
. . . is set in the underworld?
. . . involves magic?
. . . is set in France?
. . . has a map at the front?
. . . involves some kind of crime?
. . . has a boy in the leading role?
. . . could make somebody cry?
. . . is written in the 1st person?
. . . involves a trip or a journey?
. . . is over 500 words long?
. . . has a title which is seven words long?
. . . includes the death of a main character?
. . . has a prologue?
. . . has a happy ending?

. . . features a mythical beast?
. . . has a surprise ending?
. . . has at least one character falling in love?
. . . changed your perspective on something?
. . . includes some time travel?
. . . is set in the Victorian period?
. . . has a picture of some food on the front cover?
. . . made you scared at some points?
. . . deals with an aspect of war?
. . . has a one-word title?
. . . doesn't have a happy ending?
. . . involves talking animals?

Check out the Online Resources for this book for a printable checklist for your pupils.

Reading scavenger hunt

"We love it when we do a scavenger hunt. Last week I got a prize because I found all of the answers in under five minutes!"

A book scavenger hunt can be more than just fun for the children. It teaches retrieval skills, making inferences, identifying word meaning, summarising ideas and hones skimming and scanning skills.

A book scavenger hunt can be as complex or as simple as you'd like to make it. Open-ended questions and generic questions can both be used. This works well when all children have a different book to use:

Find two rhyming words on page six.
Find a description of a character.

You could also be more specific with questions. This works particularly well when all children have a whole-class copy of the same book:

Which word, on page 233, means the same as 'to lift into the air'?
How old is the junkyard dog?

Children could also be provided with a large pile of books to work their way through. This works well when giving out a large set of criteria to find. It is particularly suitable for tasks which involve things like finding the features of texts:

Can you find a subheading?
Can you find a headline?

With KS1 children, scavenger hunts can be used to help support and assess phonic knowledge. Children could be given shorter texts and a list of questions relating to phonics or spelling patterns.

Find all words with the long a sound.
Find all words which start with 'st'.
Find all words which end in 'ough'.

Read all about it!

"I love a newspaper scavenger hunt. The children are engaged, enthused, eager to read and have access to current literature."

Children's newspapers are now readily available in classrooms, alongside tablet and online versions, and provide the children with a current source of literature and language.

Here are ten activities with newspapers:

1 Preposition hunt – can the children find ten different prepositions on a double page?
2 Find the different nouns, adjectives and verbs in an article.
3 Scavenger hunt – give the children 20 questions to find the answers to.
4 Reporting clauses – how many different ways of saying 'said' are there?
5 Children should provide a partner with a summary of an article and swap some of the details. Can the children spot the one lie amongst five truths?
6 Match the headline – give out several articles along with several headlines. Can the children match the headline and story?
7 Guess the adjective – enlarge a copy of an article featuring several adjectives. Remove the adjectives and ask the children to guess the missing word.
8 Re-order the article – cut an article into individual paragraphs. Can the children read the paragraphs and put the text back together in the correct order?
9 Feature finder – use large sheets of sugar paper on the tables with the names of the features of newspapers as headings. Ask the children to cut out, and stick onto the sheets, the examples that they find.
10 Finding the 5Ws (what; why; when; where; who). Select a story and note down all of the 5Ws involved.

Teaching tip

Use several articles to create a newspaper timeline. The children should read the articles and decide, as a table, where the articles would be placed on a chronological timeline.

The restricted shelf

"Harry wandered over to the Restricted Section . . . you needed a specially signed note from one of the teachers to look in any of the restricted books . . . containing powerful Dark Magic never taught at Hogwarts . . . " – J. K. Rowling

The restricted shelf in the classroom can engage those readers who are able to read, but choose not to. The restricted shelf, just like its counterpart in the *Harry Potter* books, is for books that are not suitable for all children, but are still suitable for some of the older children in primary school.

According to the National Literacy Trust, almost one in four boys say they only read when they must, and when they do read, they can't find anything to interest them. There are many reasons for this, some of which can be found in further research from the National Literacy Trust.

If you tell the pupils that they are not allowed to read the books on the shelf because they have a swear word in them, because they are slightly rude, too violent, or because controversial things happen in them, the children will be desperate to read them. They will read them closely so that they do not miss the 'restricted' content.

This close reading will engage them in the reading process and may inspire them to read more great books.

The mystery bookshelf

"Don't judge a book by its cover!"

We're told not to judge a book by its cover, but we do. Sometimes the cover illustrations can sway us, as can the title and the blurb.

When encouraging children to read for pleasure, we sometimes need to challenge children's reading preferences. We can do this by recommending high-quality texts, as described in Idea 11. Another way of encouraging children to read beyond their preferences is to use 'The mystery bookshelf'. Cover the selected books with brown paper, so that children cannot see the title or illustrations. Children select books at random as their new reading books. Keep in mind that children may not enjoy the book they have chosen at random, and allow them to change the book without finishing it.

Write the opening line of the story on the front cover. Books with great opening lines:

- '"Where's Papa going with that axe?" said Fern to her mother as they were setting the table for breakfast.' – E. B. White, *Charlotte's Web*
- 'The Iron Man came to the top of the cliff. How far had he walked? Nobody knows.' – Ted Hughes, *The Iron Man*
- 'There was a hand in the darkness and it held a knife.' – Neil Gaiman, *The Graveyard Book*
- 'The shop from nowhere arrived with the dawn on a crisp November morning.' – Ross MacKenzie, *The Nowhere Emporium*

Taking it further

Add a short review from another child on the brown paper cover, or add key themes in a list such as:
- War
- Refugees
- Family relationships
- Loss
- Football.

Fun reading games

"Alphabetising am at good I my really sentences."

These quick-fire reading game can keep children engaged and help them to practise essential reading skills.

Alphabet sentences

Ask the children to select a sentence of over ten words from their reading books. Can they put the sentence into alphabetical order?

Syllable sieve

Ask the children to select a paragraph of text from their reading books. On a whiteboard, ask the children to create a table. They need to use four headings: one syllable, two syllables, three syllables and four or more syllables. Ask the children to work through the paragraph and record the syllables.

Follow the instructions

Give out sets of instructions to make something or to do a task. Can the children read and follow the set of instructions? Check out the Online Resources for this book for a set of instructions to use with your class.

Text jigsaw

Give out a text which involves a sequence of some kind. (See Online Resources.) Traditional tales and nursery rhymes are often good for this. Ask the children to read the text as a team; then collect it in. Cut the text into sentence strips and ask the children to place them into the correct sequence.

Reading race

Give out the same text to all children, and a list of things for them to underline in the text. The children race to find the answers and give them to the teacher.

Building blocks

Part 3

Teach grammar in context

"Building this knowledge is best achieved through a focus on grammar within the teaching of reading, writing and speaking." – Department for Education, 2013

Why teach grammar? Grammar conventions are the building blocks of reading and writing. It is for this reason that we believe that grammar is best delivered in the context of reading and writing.

Teaching tip

Children should rehearse on individual whiteboards, creating sentences to test their understanding of grammar and, when correct, use them in their writing. This skill can then be quickly revisited before each writing session within the unit.

We suggest that, once you have decided on your desired writing outcomes, look at the grammar conventions that will best achieve those outcomes. This may be done by evaluating the skills shown in previous pieces of independent writing. It may be that children need to learn the rules and conventions around apostrophe use. This can be built up through a range of writing including, in this example, fantasy narratives.

Writing narratives with fantasy creatures
The lesson flow may look a little like this:

Lesson 1 – Introduce the hero of the story.
Lesson 2 – Introduce the setting.
Lesson 3 – Hero meets the fantasy creature.
Lesson 4 – A problem develops.
Lesson 5 – The problem is resolved.

It is possible to interrupt the flow of this writing experience to work on apostrophes. However, it can be built into the process easily. In Lesson 1, demonstrate how apostrophes are needed when describing the hero, their equipment, their clothes and their characteristics.
The hero's journey started at home.
The hero's watch glowed, signalling danger.
The hero's weapon hung from his utility belt, ready for action.

This might continue in Lesson 2 where the children look at apostrophes for plurals.

Word class tennis

"Playing these games in class makes English lessons fun, and you remember it more."

Playing games around the subject of grammar allows quick repetition of a skill or concept. Adding an element of competition makes it fun and engaging. Remember to try and use the games in context wherever possible.

Knowing the four major word classes (noun, adjective, verb and adverb) is useful for writing as it allows the teacher and writer to discuss the text using technical language.

Teaching tip

Ask children to record effective responses on sticky notes to create a vocabulary wall.

Playing word class tennis
- Sit the children in pairs facing each other.
- Call out a word class, e.g. verb.
- The children then take turns to say a verb without long pauses or repeating a verb that has already been said.

Extend this idea by giving specific instructions such as 'regular past tense verbs'.

There are other variations of the game. You could give an adjective and the children pass it back and forth, following it with a noun which the adjective could accurately describe, e.g. 'terrible' could elicit responses such as:

Terrible storm
Terrible trouble
Terrible shirt

Other variations:
- Nouns beginning with a specific letter
- Adjectives to describe a specific subject
- Adverbs which describe a specific verb
- Pairs of adverbs and verbs which work well together such as: walking slowly, cautiously looking, slowly crawling, etc.
- Two adjectives that work well together to describe a certain subject.

Getting to grips with nouns

"Nouns are one of the building blocks of language and therefore essential for the children to get to grips with from an early age."

Children need to understand how to identify and how to use nouns accurately as one of the key building blocks of grammar. Once the children understand the basics, they can then move on to beginning to construct sentences accurately.

Teaching tip

Go on regular 'noun hunts' in guided reading and whole-class shared reading to strengthen understanding of nouns and their usage.

Taking it further

Look at the fact that for the final part of the lesson, some children might have suggested the park, the zoo, the shops, London, France, Alnwick Castle, etc. Together, look at how we decide whether to give a noun a capital letter, i.e. whether the noun is a general name or a specific name. Make a proper noun/ common noun grid.

Explain to the children how they can understand the meaning of the word 'noun' by showing several simple sentences with nouns missing.

Ask the children what the missing word could be. Could there be a range of different options?

- The _____was blue.

Decide together that the 'thing' that was missing could have been: sea, sky, ball, car, teddy, etc. These 'things' are nouns. Create a noun collector sheet and ask the children to move around the classroom in pairs, sleuthing for nouns to add to their noun collector sheet.

Next introduce another kind of sentence with a missing word:

- _____was happy.

Decide together that the missing word this time was probably a person's name. List these and include a capital letter. Use this as a teaching point to introduce the terms 'common noun' and 'proper noun'.

Use a final missing word sentence and ask the children to guess the omitted word.

- I went to _____.

At a later date, introduce the idea of countable and non-countable nouns.

What's my noun again?

"There's something really fun about finding out that the collective noun for rattlesnakes is a rhumba – somehow I imagine them doing a strange dance!"

Once children understand how to identify a noun, they need to move on to understand that there are different types of nouns. Having fun and playing games with grammar can help to make the concept 'stick', but can also provide information about the child's understanding.

Show the children a list of four types of nouns (common, proper, collective and abstract) and also their meanings. Can they match the four noun types with their description?

Play 'Begin at the end' with the children. Ask them to sit in pairs and give the children a noun type, e.g. common. The starting child needs to think of a common noun; the second child needs to respond with another common noun which begins with the final letter of the first word, e.g. Child 1 – table, Child 2 – egg. Children must not duplicate words. During this time, cruise the classroom to assess the children's understanding and correct misconceptions.

Once the children understand what is meant by the different noun types, explain that you are going to play the game 'Corners'. Allocate a different corner of the room for each type of noun. Have a pre-prepared list of nouns. Try not to use words that may cause confusion, e.g. bath and Bath. Ask the children to take a whiteboard and pen with them and to write 1, 2, 3 on it – these are their 'lives'. As each word is called out, ask the children to move to the appropriate corner. Those children standing in the wrong corner need to remove one of their lives. The game should be played until a winner or winners are found.

Teaching tip

Ask the children to classify their nouns into countable and non-countable nouns.

Taking it further

Ask the children to research collective nouns. Give them an A-Z of animals and ask them to research the collective noun for each animal. They could also reverse the task and find the animal to match a collective noun given by you.

'Guess Who' with expanded noun phrases

"'But I don't understand how to write a jaw-droppingly good expanded noun phrase,' he muttered."

Being able to craft well-written expanded noun phrases is like being able to decorate a cake. They add interest for the reader and make the sentence 'taste' altogether better.

Teaching tip

Use a grid to record expanded noun phrases which determine how the noun has been modified, e.g. prepositional phrase, adjectival phrase, etc.

Whether it be in non-fiction or fiction writing, the expanded noun phrase will be an integral part of the text. Getting children to recognise them in reading is the first step in getting them to be able to write them. Begin by asking children to notice the nouns and noun phrases they read in the texts they are exposed to, and also to identify the words/phrases which modify the noun at the head of the phrase:

*On his hand sat a **small, red** dragon **with unusually bright eyes**.*

Give out or display a grid of different creatures, in a similar format to the popular game 'Guess Who?' to make this challenging for the children. Use one theme for all of the pictures, e.g. dragons. Ask the children to play in pairs. The children need to select an image and try to guess their opponent's image by asking yes/no questions using expanded noun phrases:

Is it a bright red dragon? Is it a dragon with spikes on its head?

Once the children have guessed who their opponent's character is, they can begin to construct some expanded noun phrases about the other characters in the grid.

Accurate adjectives

"I've used eight adjectives to describe the car, so that means it must be good writing, right?"

By using these quick and easy games, children can learn how to use adjectives well, and where less is more.

Select one pupil to come out to the front, and ask them to turn to face the remainder of the class, away from the board. Display an image on the board. The children in the audience need to help the child to guess what the image is by offering adjectives to describe it. This is where the children need to be taught that precision of adjectives is important. It is not enough to say 'big' as both a car and a planet could be described as big, though one is obviously much larger than the other. Encourage the children not to repeat adjectives. The child who is guessing the image on the board needs to ask at least six children before making a guess. It would be advisable to note down some of the children's responses and to also allow thesauruses to be used.

A further game to encourage use of a wider range of adjectives is 'Double trouble'. Ask the children to sit in pairs, and distribute the same image to each child. This can also be played as a whole class by using one image displayed on the board. Give the children two minutes (this could be altered) to write down as many adjectives to describe the image as possible. This works well with images of one item, e.g. a tree, an ice-cream or a butterfly. At the end of the two minutes, the children should take it in turns (if playing as a pair) to call out an adjective. If their player also has the word, then both players need to cross out the adjective. This should continue until both children are left with words that their opponent doesn't have.

Taking it further

Ask the children to use their well-selected adjectives to write a description of the item(s) in the image.

Verbs – don't let them make you tense!

"Children will often utter the words 'runned' or 'taked'. Getting them to orally repeat words, using the correct verb tenses, will help to improve this skill in writing."

Getting it right, from the start, is essential to children's progress in grammar. Habits are often formed from an early age and can continue into adulthood. By using this 'little and often' approach, children can quickly start to understand the rules of verb tenses and what to do with irregular verbs.

Tell the children that you are going to have a 'verb showdown' with the children as they work throughout the day. This should continue throughout the year, particularly with words that seem to be consistently confused or irregular verbs.

Agree a colour for different tenses. This is an easily differentiated activity by adding more tenses. However, to begin with, it is advised that past, present and future tenses are enough. Create a PowerPoint, or similar, with several different verbs ready for the children. The first slide should display the verb in black; the next slide should be a single colour – this is the cue for the children to change the tense, giving their answers orally or using a whiteboard. The children need to change the word into the tense you have selected. You may need to begin by having the words 'past tense' also written on the slide. As the children get used to the colours, they will become faster at the process.

This simple activity can be carried out at various points throughout the day and can begin to feed into the children's writing. It would be useful if the whole school adopted consistent tense colours as this could help with marking and peer-/self-assessment.

Bonus idea ★

While marking a piece of writing, you could highlight to a child that their tenses are muddled by simply circling the verb and then underlining in the colour of the correct tense.

How, where and when?

"Darth Vader very rarely ate unhealthily and enjoyed exercising after dark."

As teachers, we often ask children to give us more information and more detail in their writing. By highlighting the role of adverbs, and teaching how to identify them, children can begin to really consider the information that they give the reader, and how they can manipulate clauses to better effect.

Clarify the role of an adverbial phrase. Talk together about the fact that an adverbial phrase answers the questions: how, where and/or when. Can they identify the difference between an adverb and an adverbial phrase? Do the children understand that some adverbial phrases contain adverbs, whilst others do not? Show a series of adverbs, adverbial phrases and non-adverbial phrases on an interactive whiteboard, or similar. Explain that you want to keep the adverbial phrases, but you want to throw the other things away. Ask the children to shout 'throw' or 'keep' as they see each word or phrase, e.g. quietly (throw), very slowly (keep), extremely delicious (throw).

Share a selection of images where the children can clearly see a verb taking place. Ask the children to write a sentence on their whiteboards to explain what is happening. Next, shout either 'manner', 'time' or 'place'. The children need to come up with the ending to the sentence using the appropriate adverbial phrase. To keep the children's interest in the task, use a variety of images they might be familiar with, such as Harry Potter flying on a broomstick.

Manner (how) – with great care.
Time (when) – just before his potions lesson.
Place (where) – over the Quidditch pitch.

Teaching tip

Use sections of text to look for adverbial phrases and carry out a 'phrase swap'. The children should swap each phrase they find for another which doesn't alter the meaning.

Taking it further

Look at how these adverbial phrases can be moved to the opening position in the sentence. Can the children construct sentences using all three types of adverbial phrase?

Silly sentences – adverbs of frequency

"I always eat the toilet paper. I never brush the hippopotamus!"

By using these quick and easy games, children can learn how to use adverbs of frequency and also realise that not all adverbs end in '-ly'.

Teaching tip

Use adverbs of indefinite frequency to begin with. Once these are understood, change to adverbs of definite frequency, such as hourly, daily, etc. Look at their positioning. These adverbs usually come at the end of the sentence.

An engaging start to a lesson about adverbs is to ask the children to have a competition to list as many adverbs as they can, but they should only list those which DON'T end in -ly. The children's natural response will be to begin to list adverbs of manner ending '-ly'. Encourage them to remember what an adverb is, and then begin to build a list of adverbs of manner, time, place or degree. Use books to look for where a verb has been modified by an adverb. Try dividing the task by tables to focus on one adverb type each.

A fun way to introduce adverbs of frequency is to create funny sentences. Before the lesson, prepare a set of cards per table (or download them from the Online Resources for this book). Each table needs around ten adverbs of frequency, 20 common nouns with articles (the dog, an apple, etc.) and 20 verbs in the present tense (be careful about verb selection!). The children then need to begin to build sentences by randomly selecting cards from each pile and replacing them once they have been used. Word repetition is fine, though encourage the children to make swaps if they constantly draw the same cards. Each sentence must start with 'I'. There can be some hilarious outcomes, e.g. 'I often paint the lion', 'I regularly walk the laptop'. Ask the children to record these in their books and then play again.

Most bestest comparative and superlative adjectives

"We loved competing in the Classroom Olympics! Noah did the longest sprout roll and I had the widest mouth!"

How many times have you heard the words, 'most bestest' or 'more betterer'? These simple mistakes are made through a misunderstanding of comparative and superlative adjectives. With these games, the children can play with language and learn the grammatical rules at the same time.

Ask three pupils to come to the front of the class with whiteboards. Put the children in height order without explaining what you are doing. Write the word 'tall' on the far left board. Move to the second child and ask the class to guess what word you are going to write on the board. When this has been ascertained (taller), move on to the final board. On a large board, create a three-column table with the headings 'adjective, comparative adjective, superlative adjective'. Can the children think of other adjectives to find the comparative and superlative forms for, e.g. 'near', 'nearer', 'nearest'?

Are there any that don't follow the pattern? These words tend to be over six letters or more than two syllables long, such as 'important' and 'interesting'. In these cases, the adjective uses 'more' and 'most'. Can the children think of any irregular comparative adjectives which don't follow these rules at all, such as 'good' and 'bad'.

Ask the children to work as a table to create comparative and superlative sentences to describe their peers, e.g. 'James has longer hair than Taz, but Anita has the longest hair'. Set the children some challenges to see if they can use some more difficult adjectives.

Taking it further

Show the children the Guinness World Records website. You will need to make a free account first. Search some of the records and look at the format of the descriptions. Can the children spot the comparative and superlative language? Hold a 'Classroom Olympics' (these could be funny tasks and not necessarily sporting) and ask the children to write up the results as entries for the Class Records book.

Cut and jumble

"It wasn't until I physically gave the children the sentence strips to cut up that they could actually see how the clauses could be manipulated."

This is such a simple idea and can be invaluable in getting the children to understand how to re-order sentences.

Give out long strips of paper and ask the children to write a complex sentence on each. Remind them that a complex sentence uses an independent (or main) clause and at least one subordinate clause. It would perhaps be wise to give the children several examples and ask them to identify the different clauses.

> *When the bell rang, the children ran to grab their coats.*

> *She bit her nails while waiting for the phone to ring.*

To begin with, ask the children to cut the strips between the clauses (this may need some practice) and move the clauses into the opposite positions. Look at how the positioning can change. Challenge the children to add an additional clause.

> *The children, **who were eager to go out to play**, ran to grab their coats when the bell rang.*

Look at what happens with the use of the comma. How does it change? Next, challenge the children to add adverbs and adjectives, reminding them not to add too many.

> *The **noisy** children, who were **rather** eager to go out to play, ran to grab their coats when the school bell rang.*

Repeat the process several times and simplify or extend as needed.

Prepositional phrases in disguise

"The prepositional phrase was hidden in the text, below the heading, at the end of the sentence."

By encouraging the children to identify and use prepositional phrases as adverbs or adjectives, the teacher is also helping the child to understand what the prepositional phrase is modifying.

Begin by giving the children an image of a busy scene, e.g. *The Funeral of a Viking* by Sir Francis Bernard Dicksee. Ask the children to imagine the sounds which would be audible in such a scene.

Crashing, shouting, crackling, roaring, etc.

Ask the children to give you phrases containing the verb at the head. The verb could change to past tense.

Crashing **against the beach**
Exploding **on the horizon**

Explain that here, the prepositional phrases are acting as an adverb as they are modifying the verb. There are also prepositional phrases which act like adjectives to modify a noun.

The men **in the water**
The crowds **on the beach**

Next, give out an image in the middle of the table and two piles of different-coloured strips of paper. Split the table and ask half of the children to come up with prepositional phrases as adverbs and the other half to produce prepositional phrases as adjectives. Once the children have done this, they can build sentences using either form of the prepositional phrase or both, e.g.

The crowds on the beach surged towards the boat whilst singing and chanting songs to Odin.

Teaching tip

Ensure the children understand the rules of placement of prepositional phrases. Look at a selection of misplaced prepositional phrases to help the children to see where they can or cannot be moved within a sentence.

Punctuation power – colons

"Colons can be used for many things: introducing, explaining, extending and amplifying."

Ensuring the children have a good grasp of dependent and independent clauses is essential to being able to work with colons and semicolons.

One of the uses of a colon is as a piece of punctuation which introduces additional detail – kind of like a writerly form of 'ta-dah!' or a signpost to extra information. The children need to understand that the information before the colon must be an independent clause. They also need to understand that the information following the colon needs to explain or support the initial clause in the sentence.

Several items are required for the visit: a waterproof coat, wellington boots and a packed lunch.

Provide the children with the endings to colon sentences. Ask them what might have gone before the colon, e.g.

: the boat wasn't big enough for six people.

It was then that he delivered the dreadful news: the boat wasn't big enough for six people.

Then play 'Race against the clock'. Give out a sheet of paper to each table, with colon sentence openings or endings written on it. Explain that the children need to work as a team and think of the missing information for each sentence. As an additional challenge, ask them to write independent colon sentences. Limit the amount of time for the groups to complete the tasks.

Punctuation power – semicolons

"I never use semicolons in my writing; some punctuation is just so difficult to place."

Semicolons are one of the most underused pieces of punctuation. They are feared by adults, misused by children and confused across the board. By using some simple tricks and games, the children can become more confident in understanding their rules and more adept at using them.

Introduce the idea that a semicolon separates two independent clauses, and ask for several volunteers to come to the front of the class. Explain the semicolon as a break in a sentence where BOTH clauses are independent. This is not the only use; however, to teach all uses at once can be confusing for the children. Next, explain that semicolons need to separate ideas in a sentence which are linked or have a relationship in some way.

Give out an array of independent clauses which could be joined with a semi-colon (see Online Resources for some ready-made sentences). You should also add in a few dependent clauses as 'red herrings'. Ask the children to get up and move around the classroom to find their partner.

- *It was an incredibly hot day; our ice-creams melted within minutes.*
- *The tiger escaped from the zoo; safety checks on the enclosures were poor.*
- *Because it was unusually quiet.* (Dependent)

Did anyone not have a partner? Make a list of pairings, and write them on the board with a semicolon between. Then ask the children to change the dependent clauses to independent clauses. Can they then place these within a sentence containing a semicolon?

> **Teaching tip**
>
> Use the teaching of semicolons to help the children understand what a comma splice is.

Punctuation power – ellipses

"Ellipses are so much more than just a duh-duh-duhhh!"

Ellipses are one of the least taught pieces of punctuation. Many children see them only as a way of adding suspense and tension to the end of a story.

Teaching tip

Encourage the children to be selective about the way in which they are using their ellipses, and ensure they understand what other features help to build suspense and tension.

The first thing to say about the use of ellipses is that they should be used sparingly. They are the cherry on the cake, not the butter in the mixture. Give the children a piece of text littered with ellipses (see Online Resources). It is key that they see that overuse of the punctuation can hinder the flow and sometimes alter the meaning of the text. Can the children tidy up the work? Which ellipses are extraneous? Then get to the nitty-gritty of the ellipses. What roles do they perform? Can they identify the role by simply looking at the sentence?

- Showing pauses in dialogue or that dialogue is incomplete:
  'Hold on . . . the ambulance is on its way . . . just hold on!' he yelled.
- Indicating an omission in the narrative:
  Bang! Bang! There it was again . . . she froze.
- Showing the trailing-off of a thought:
  Now where did I put my . . .
- Implying something is to follow:
  The snake drew its head back to a striking position and then lunged at his arm . . .
- Putting emphasis on the next word:
  Her eyes grew wide, and her jaw dropped as she saw them . . . diamonds.
- Shortening a quote:
  'You have only begun to discover your power . . . we can end this destructive conflict and bring order to the galaxy.'

Ask the children to watch a short clip which includes tension. Can they practise their use of ellipses by creating a short piece of text to describe the scene?

Punctuation power – speech marks

"Using knock-knock jokes really helped the children begin to see how to punctuate dialogue."

Teaching children how to accurately punctuate speech can be made much easier by following these simple activities.

Watch a short clip where two characters are having a discussion. Identify what each character has said by using two different colours of paper and writing the words spoken by each character into a speech bubble. Next, stick the speech bubbles onto one side of the board, in order, under one another. This should help the children to see the point that each new speaker needs a new line. Add speech marks to the paper so that the children can see that they contain the dialogue only. Then, on the opposite side of the board, begin to write out the dialogue using speech marks and two different colours. Introduce the idea of a reporting clause – keep it simple at first. Point out that the dialogue will have a piece of punctuation before the speech marks close. Write the response to the first line of dialogue, then stop.

> 'My favourite flavour of ice-cream is chocolate,' said Batman.
> 'I quite like strawberry,' replied Robin.

Allow the children to practise these first two steps with the rest of the text before becoming more technical. Move on to look at other punctuation and allow the children to rehearse accordingly. To apply the use of question marks and exclamation marks, use knock-knock jokes.

> 'Knock-knock,' said Batman.
> 'Who's there?' asked Robin.
> 'Figs,' answered Batman.
> 'Figs who?' questioned Robin.
> 'Figs the doorbell, it's broken!' laughed Batman.

Teaching tip

Make sure the children know that speech marks, inverted commas and quotation marks are all names for the punctuation marks which go around direct speech.

Punctuation power – match and win

"I love playing match and win in class because it's fun and it makes me think about the job that the punctuation does."

Games like these help children to consolidate and apply their knowledge of punctuation. They also provide the teacher with important assessment information and can be easily differentiated according to ability.

Taking it further

Ask the children to sit in pairs. Using the same punctuation cards, play a game of 'Snap!' with a twist. When two matching cards are found, the players need to use a whiteboard, or similar, to write a correctly-punctuated sentence featuring that piece of punctuation. Whoever wins the challenge, in the fastest time, wins ten points. Play for an agreed amount of time or until one player reaches a target number.

Create punctuation cards for each child. Use a 4 x 4 grid and include three full stops, two commas, two exclamation marks, two question marks, a semicolon, a colon, a dash, an ellipsis, an apostrophe, brackets and speech marks. Cut along the grid lines to create 16 individual cards. You will also need to prepare sentences with two pieces of missing punctuation in each – ensure there is a full range and a variety of sentence types. Give each child a deck of the cards and ask them to shuffle them. Display the first sentence to the class and ask the children to pull out the first **two** cards from the top of their pile. If both cards are a match for the missing punctuation, then the child scores ten points. If one of the cards is a match for one of the pieces of missing punctuation, then the child scores five points. If the child has no matching cards, then they have the opportunity to earn bonus points by using a whiteboard to create a sentence using **both** pieces of punctuation from the top of their deck. If it is correctly punctuated, then the child scores five points. Play several rounds and allow time to rectify any misconceptions.

Synonym snowballs

"When I find a new word, I just add it to the synonym stockpile."

This activity is one which can be set up at the beginning of the year and then added to as the year progresses. Using this fun activity, the children can create and store synonyms.

Pre-prepare an A4 sheet of paper for each child with an adjective or verb on it – select words which could be improved, e.g. happy, little, old. Explain the snowball fight rules and that the children need to aim for the desks, not one another. You could also put something in the middle of a table as a target for the children to throw their snowballs into. Explain that the children should think of an alternative word, with the same or similar meaning, to the word on the paper, and then write it somewhere on the sheet, e.g. worried – anxious. After the children have written their word, ask them to crumple the paper into a 'snowball' and throw to another table. This should be repeated several times with each child adding to the snowball. The children are not allowed to repeat words, and if they find the task difficult, they should be allowed to access a thesaurus or similar. As an extension, ask the children to create a sentence which includes the synonym. You could also set a time limit and ask the children to write as many synonyms on the paper as they can in the allotted time before throwing it to the next table.

Teaching tip

Following the activity, create a 'synonym stockpile' for the classroom. Use plastic wallets in a binder to store the sheets or transfer the words onto a new sheet to add to the wallet.

Taking it further

The same activity could be used at the beginning of a topic or before a piece of writing. Extra sheets can be added as needed, and exciting new vocabulary can be transferred from children's writing, shared writing and modelled writing. The words could also be transferred into a Word document, or similar, to be shared electronically.

5Ws fold down

"I really loved creating our own stories to write the orientation for."

Using this fun activity, the children create the news story for their orientations.

I absolutely love this game. It can have some hilarious results and is fun to play while looking at journalistic writing.

1 Give out long strips of paper.
2 The children should play the game as a table. Ask them to put their name on the back, at the bottom.
3 Each child should take their strip of paper and write the name of a person, or character, at the top of the paper (the paper should be portrait). This is their WHO.
4 Next, they should fold the paper over twice so that their answer is no longer visible.
5 Then they should pass the paper to the person on their right.
6 Next, the children should write a WHAT clue. This could be anything, and the children are often very inventive with their suggestions.
7 Again, they should fold the paper so their answer cannot be seen and pass the paper on to the right.
8 This should continue with WHERE, WHEN and WHY – tell them to be more general with the WHY. On a table of fewer than five, this will involve an extra pass. The children should then pass the list back to the owner for them to be unveiled.

The results can be hilarious:
Mickey Mouse
Ate a mouldy sandwich
In the cloakroom
At midnight
Because he liked it.

Writing

Part 4

Thematic learning

"Where a thematic approach has achieved great success, we have often seen schools use one book for all subjects. Children don't see their learning as a disjointed, disconnected process – rather, a continuum of learning."

Many schools take a thematic approach to the curriculum, building links between subjects and allowing children a deeper immersion in different areas. In those schools where English and other subjects are kept as separate entities, vital learning opportunities are often missed.

Taking it further

Use high-quality books and films to theme the learning.

Where schools take a thematic approach, English is linked to the wider curriculum, and language acquisition goes hand in hand with the development of subject knowledge. When links across subjects are made, there are opportunities to develop knowledge of the topic through related texts in English and to acquire new language and practise skills in context.

When immersed in a topic, children are exposed to subject-specific vocabulary. Whilst studying the Ancient Greeks, for example, children will hear and read: democracy, trireme, Sparta, etc. which could be then used to enhance writing across the whole curriculum. This also enables the children to compose text with authorial expertise about a subject – something we talk about in Idea 75.

Thematic approaches to the curriculum can also help to support narrative writing. If we stay with the example of the Greeks, then writing an action scene based upon Troy would be very difficult without an understanding of that time period. Where knowledge is poor or inaccurate, children often find the writing process difficult and the quality of the work they produce can suffer.

Experience is key

"I've never even been to a park here in England."

Imagine having to write about something that you have no experience of. Not just that you haven't physically been there — Antarctica, for example — but you've never read about it, seen photographs of it or experienced it through film or television. Even if you're an experienced writer, you would find it difficult. Now imagine how some of our young novice writers feel.

First-hand experiences are vital. If you are writing about castles, try to take your class to a castle, and importantly, carry out some writing activities while you are there. It may be that some of your children have not been to a large city before or have never visited a beach. Go and spend the day in the city or on the sands. Discuss the smells, sights, sounds and found objects.

Obviously, all experiences cannot come from primary sources. A trip to the Great Exhibition of 1851 at Crystal Palace would be an impossibility, as would chartering a flight to deep space for your science fiction unit. Use secondary sources for these experiences; visit museums, and engage actors and experts to come into school. Support these experiences with films and books.

A word of caution: do not rely solely on written accounts because, for some children, it is difficult to create images in their mind from written accounts of something that they lack experience of. In these cases, they often rearrange the written accounts and deliver them back to you.

Taking it further

There are a number of virtual reality programs available which allow pupils to 'visit' a number of locations from the comfort of their classroom. One great experience that schools can take advantage of is Google Expeditions. (https://edu.google.com/expeditions/)

Unusual narrative stimuli

"My class absolutely loved the fact we started the unit by using the Big Bad Wolf's Facebook profile!"

Pique the children's interest with a range of unusual stimuli.

Teaching tip

Check out www.classtools.net/FB/homepage to create fake Facebook pages for the characters in a story.

1 **Drama props used to create a character**
   Consider what you want the children to find out about the protagonist/antagonist!

2 **Create a 'crime scene' in the classroom**
   Creating a crime scene so that the children can pick over the clues can be extremely rewarding. (See Idea 46.)

3 **Problem pages**
   Create a letter from Bess, the landlord's daughter, explaining her love for the Highwayman.

4 **Speech bubbles**
   Consider the conversation between two characters and create speech bubbles for the children to use as a stimulus.

5 **Journalistic stimulus**
   Create a newspaper report about an incident for the children to turn into a narrative.

6 **Social media updates**
   Use a classroom social media profile for a character and share it with the children.

7 **Dramatic start**
   Invite the children into the classroom to 'witness a scene' between characters.

8 **Using artwork**
   Invite the children to evaluate, interpret and respond to a work before creating an imaginative narrative piece.

Bonus idea ★

Combine some of the techniques mentioned here to provide the children with a wide-ranging starting point for their writing.

Physical hooks to inspire writing

"What lesson is this, Sir? We are supposed to be doing English."

A giant egg — what will hatch from it? A flashing box in the middle of the floor — what's inside? Bubbles floating around the classroom — who can catch one?

Imagine you are planning on using a narrative in English in which a magic box plays a major role. The week before, a box is delivered to your class wrapped in brown paper and addressed to the children, but with a warning that it shouldn't be opened before a specific date. All children enjoy getting parcels, which means that they will be excited about opening this one. Allow them to take turns at guessing daily. They will enjoy debating the content with each other, and their imaginations will go into overdrive. By the time the day of the opening comes along, they will have already formed narratives in their minds. When they encounter a mysterious box in the narrative which they are studying, then they will know exactly how the character who opens the box is feeling at that point.

Linking experiences to texts will allow children to connect their concrete experiences with the abstract within the films and texts which they are studying. You could try:

- A giant egg — what will hatch from it?
- An old battered suitcase with the initials H.P. on it — what is inside?
- A bag of costume jewellery — where have they come from?
- An old letter sealed with wax — what is inside?

Teaching tip

Sometimes the removal of an object from the classroom can engage and enthuse the children as much as adding something can. Who stole Mrs Hardy's chair? Where has the class bear gone?

The crime scene

"The children were really excited, and even the more reluctant children were eager to get involved."

A powerful and exciting narrative hook for pupils of all ages is the involvement in a crime scene investigation. It can sometimes take a little organising but the benefits for imaginative speaking and listening are great.

The crime scene investigation is a great 'jumping off point' for a range of writing genres such as mystery, adventure or historical fiction. It allows children to engage in discussions around the narrative by creating hypotheses and predictions.

Setting up your crime scene
Decide upon the narrative that you would like as your focus. Introduce the scenario to the pupils. If looking at 'The Highwayman' by Alfred Noyes, for example, introduce the premise that a crime has been committed and that two people have ended up dead. Provide children with evidence packs. It is exciting for them to handle real artefacts, but if these are difficult to source, photographs will suffice.

Ask children if they can link any of the clues together. In the case of 'The Highwayman', you may want to provide: a tricorn hat; an old key; a bag of coins and jewellery; an image of a pistol; some old love letters; a red ribbon; a bundle of lace; and some hay.

In groups, the children should discuss how these clues could be linked and begin to generate narratives. If studying a written text, you can introduce sections of text as 'witness testimony' in order to reinforce the children's burgeoning narratives.

A walk in sound

"The three great elemental sounds in nature are the sound of rain, the sound of wind in a primeval wood, and the sound of outer ocean on a beach." – Henry Beston

What does falling rain sound like? How does this change as it hits broad leaves and runs down onto the rainforest floor, creating streams and rivers? These are questions a good writer will be able to answer through their descriptive writing.

If we want our children to be able to effectively describe sounds to add to the experience of the reader, then they will have had to have experience of the sounds.

When introducing pre-recorded sounds, ask the children to close their eyes in order to sharpen their senses. Allow them to listen to the track through for the first time before asking generic questions such as: Where are you? What do you think is there? What could be happening?

You may want to prompt them as the sounds play, asking a range of rhetorical questions to direct their attentions to key sounds.

Some questions to ask:

- What is making that noise? What colour is it?
- What is up in the sky? How is it moving?
- What are you walking on? How does it feel?
- Is it light or dark?
- How would you describe, using words, the softness of this sound?
- Can you tell where you are, from the sounds?
- How do you feel in this place?

Children can record their responses and peer review them in order to use them in their narrative writing.

Taking it further

Create a soundscape using untuned and tuned percussion, alongside sounds that the children can make with their bodies and their mouths, to represent different settings. Record them and play back for analysis.

Build a picture

"Our teacher gave us the most amazing picture. My section had an octopus crawling through the wreck of a boat. I couldn't wait to write about it!"

Teachers often use visual stimuli to support the writing process. However, using an image and splitting it into several sections allows the children to focus in on fewer details, refine their descriptions and consider how their work complements the work of others.

Find an interesting image. This activity works best with a 'busy' image, but you can challenge pupils by using images with some 'empty' spaces. Split the image by drawing a grid over it. 2 x 2 or 3 x 2 fit easily into classroom groups. 9 x 9 presents more difficulties, but you could have some children within the group writing descriptions for more than one section. This activity could also be carried out using a frame from a film or animation.

Allocate sections and allow children time to develop descriptions of their own section before sharing these with the rest of the group. To stretch some learners, give them specific success criteria such as:

• Use a simile or metaphor.
• Use personification to describe an inanimate object.
• Start a sentence with a verb.
• Develop expansion before and after a noun.
• Use a relative clause.

Bonus idea ★

In order to create a cohesive piece of writing, it might be prudent to create a class vocabulary bank prior to carrying out the individual descriptions.

Once they are completed, arrange the descriptions onto a large sheet of paper to mirror those in the original image. Children then choose in which order to use the descriptions to create their individual pieces. Share the finished pieces so children can compare the similarities and differences between their writing from the same image.

Map out the story

"The world is not in your books and maps, it's out there." –
J. R. R. Tolkien

Tolkien may have had Gandalf say that the world is not to be found in a book, but this is one occasion where Gandalf is wrong – sort of. There are many worlds to be found in books; many books begin with their whole world on a page and open with a map. A map can be a great starting point for discussing narrative with children.

Children can create their own narrative from the information on a map.

You could use a map from a great novel such as *Oliver and the Seawigs* by Philip Reeve or *Sea* by Sarah Driver (from 'The Huntress Trilogy'). There is a multitude of books with maps to choose from.

Before reading the story, children can predict what they think each location will be like and what will happen there. After reading, children can use the map to create their own mini-adventures based on the characters in the book, or they could import their own characters into the setting. Children can create their own maps. An outline of an island or a kingdom can become the basis for an original narrative. Children can work alone or as part of a group to decide what can be found in their newly-discovered land, perhaps:

- a waterfall — smuggler's cove
- a dark cave — a deep well
- an abandoned cottage — the Forest of Doom
- a castle — the Bridge of Hope.

Descriptions can then be developed for each location and used in the narratives with a range of different characters.

Teaching tip

Find more story books with maps, search for the hashtag #bookswithmaps on Twitter.

Taking it further

Some children may struggle to describe the locations just from a line drawing. They could be supported with photographic images or illustrations, in addition to the map outline.

Once upon a time . . . the art of the opening

"I think 'Once upon a time . . . ' is ok, but now I try to dip the reader into my story with a bit more excitement."

There is a range of ways in which to capture the reader's imagination in an opening passage, from grabbing their attention in the first line to leaving them hanging with the last line, desperate for more.

Teaching tip

Create your own list of excellent openings with the children by taking a sample of texts from the school library and asking the children to sort them into categories based on their opening paragraphs. The children could then write their own versions, using the category headings.

Ask your average six to seven-year-old to tell you a story and they often come out with one of the following opening lines:

- In a land far away . . .
- It was a dark and stormy night . . .
- There was once a boy who . . .

Here are five creative ways to open a story:

Describe the setting
'It was a dark, blustery afternoon in spring, and the city of London was chasing a small mining town across the dried-out bed of the old North Sea.' This is the opening line from Philip Reeves' *Mortal Engines*; it describes the setting and leaves the reader's head filled with many questions about this strange landscape.

Character description
C. S. Lewis opens *The Voyage of the Dawn Treader* by introducing Eustace: 'There was a boy called Eustace Clarence Scrubb, and he almost deserved it.' This single line sums up how the reader will feel about Eustace after reading the opening chapters of the story. When we first hear of Mary Lennox in *The Secret Garden*, we hear that 'Everybody said she was the most disagreeable-looking child ever seen', and as the story unfolds, we see that Mary isn't the nicest of children.

In the middle of the action

'There was a hand in the darkness, and it held a knife' is the opening line to *The Graveyard Book* by Neil Gaiman. This short and simple line transports the reader straight into the darkness and into the action. This method can also be demonstrated through film, as seen in the French short film *Replay* by Talantis. As the film opens, we see a young woman running for the safety of a bunker in a barren landscape. We do not know who she is, where she is running from, or where she is going to. All of this is revealed later, but the audience is hooked from the first shot.

Dialogue

When Fern asks her mother, 'Where's Papa going with that axe?' at the beginning of E. B. White's *Charlotte's Web*, the reader is left wondering what he will be doing with the axe. When her mother replies, 'Out to the hoghouse . . . Some pigs were born last night' then it becomes clear what Father is going to be doing and, as readers, we are shocked and want to find out if the pigs are saved.

Make the reader wonder

There are many ways to make a reader wonder. You could use a statement that makes the reader form questions as in *Rooftoppers* by Katherine Rundell: 'On the morning of its first birthday, a baby was found floating in a cello case in the middle of the English Channel.' The reader is left wondering: Who is this baby? Has it been abandoned? How long has it been there? How did it get there? What will happen to it? Why is it in a cello case? A direct question asked by a first-person narrator can have a similar effect. Michael Lawrence's opening line to *The Toilet of Doom* reads, 'Ever had the feeling your life's been flushed down the toilet?' This evokes a response from the reader and makes them wonder what is so bad that the narrator thinks this.

Taking it further

Compare the openings of books with film openings. Watch a number of film openings with the children and see if they can match them to the examples they have seen in books.

Unpicking paragraphs to use as a model

"I rely heavily upon picking apart paragraphs and demonstrating to the children why an author has made these choices."

Sometimes we read a paragraph and wish that we could have written it ourselves. As teachers of writing, we share these texts and specific paragraphs with children to show them what a good one looks like (WAGOLL).

Teaching tip

Develop this method of outlining each sentence – sometimes referred to as 'slow writing' – to create paragraphs which rehearse specific skills.

So, what happens when we give the children a WAGOLL? Do they know how to unpick the contents in order to recreate the success in their own writing? As teachers, we need still to model this.

In *Danny, the Champion of the World* by Roald Dahl, there is a tense passage at the beginning of Chapter 8 – 'The Pit', where Danny is alone in the woods, looking for his father. If we unpick the model, we can see how Roald Dahl has created such a great piece of writing.

The first sentence is a first-person description which also gives an indication of the time. The second adds detail to the description by using a simile. Next comes description of movement. In the fourth sentence, a single word is used repeatedly for emphasis: 'I listened and listened'. This is followed by a short sentence which describes the action. There is a lull in the tension as we get a long description of the woods and creatures. This is followed by another sentence which repeats the key word 'listening'. This is followed by personification of the silence. The paragraph ends with a short repetitive sentence, reinforcing how quiet everything was in the darkness.

Pupils can create their own sentence using these models, applying them to their own characters and settings.

Think it, stick it

"Each day of our lives we make deposits in the memory banks of our children." – Charles R. Swindoll

When building up to a piece of writing over a period of days, we work on developing character, setting and plot before pulling these strands together in an extended piece. Through discussion, the children share wonderful ideas, but often by the time the completed piece is finished, many of the great ideas are sadly absent.

If you can, encourage the children to record their ideas throughout the week to use at a later point. A 'writer's journal' or jotter could be used to record these ideas, but not all schools subscribe to an additional 'ideas book' and only have their more formal English exercise books in which writing down a single line or idea for a narrative is discouraged.

As an alternative, or in addition to, a jotter, children can use 'sticky notes' to record their ideas. They can be used quickly and stuck on or inside exercise books. They can also be shared on the 'ideas wall' to inspire others.

Using 'sticky notes' in this way can enhance the writing process, allowing children to collate their 'best' ideas ready to be included in their writing and also allowing them to easily edit or reject these ideas too.

The 'Post-it Plus' app allows the teacher or pupil to easily photograph and collect these ideas for digital storage. On the app, they can be rotated, enlarged, grouped, labelled and shared easily. They can be shared on a digital whiteboard and accessed by pupils, individually or collaboratively.

Taking it further

Padlet is an online virtual 'bulletin' board on which children and teachers can collaborate, reflect and share easily. Children can create their own walls, and teachers can create group and class walls to post ideas. Check out www.padlet.com.

Building narrative characters

"How often have you read a child's work about a little boy called Harry with magical powers?"

Creating a believable main character for a narrative is imperative to the reader's enjoyment of the story. Children will often rely upon the characters they have read and seen, as a person to base their own characters on, but writing an original character is not that difficult.

Many teachers begin by asking, 'What does the character look like?'. Whereas, the first question should be, 'What will they do in the story?'. Ask the children to consider what their role will be in the story by creating a timeline of events which the character will be involved in. Then, at each of the points marked on the timeline, consider the character's traits and how he/she will behave. Next, consider a main scene for the character. Hot seat the children, in groups, so that they can explain, in character, what they will do during these scenes. Begin to consider what the character looks like. Complete a visible/invisible chart. Explain that we can see that a character wears glasses; however, we can't see that they had an eye operation as a child.

When we start to write

- Main characters do not need to be perfect; they can have flaws.
- Use 'show, don't tell' to give some details about the character: *The settee groaned beneath him.*
- Use the senses to describe details about the character: *She had that funny, musty smell about her, like the bottom of an old handbag.*
- Focus on the extraordinary: *It was clear she wasn't quite the same as 'normal' children because she glowed in the moonlight.*
- Show the character through dialogue.
- Show the character through their values.
- Talk about what they always/never do.

Hot seating v2.0

"I am Henry VIII; I had six wives and I am really fat!"

Hot seating is a widely-used drama technique, particularly useful for developing understanding of a character's background, behaviour and motivation. Here it gets an upgrade.

Before beginning the hot seating session, pupils should record the questions that they would like to ask. Remind them about the differences between open and closed questioning. For the purposes of this activity, open ended-questions are more effective for generating ideas.

When it is time for the hot seating, model the role of the character interviewee. Props and costumes may be used in order to enhance the experience.

One of the drawbacks to traditional single hot seating is that not all children get the opportunity to experience being in role. Another is that if there are lots of questions asked during the sessions, then the answers are not easily recalled during the writing process. This is where hot seating needs to get an upgrade through the use of 'modern technology' and become hot seating v2.0.

The simplest way of saving the responses to be used later is to record them using a video camera. However, by using some specifically-tailored apps, children can actually become the characters and have their words spoken by them. Apps such as YAKiT Kids, Morpho Booth and Chatterpix allow pupils to quickly become the character. The Puppet Pals app allows both the interviewer and interviewee to record their words and play them back. Once saved, these short films can be used in multiple sessions to support writing.

> **Teaching tip**
>
> For some pupils, a single hot seat at the front of the class can be a little daunting. Hot seating in small groups, or with a partner, may be more productive.

> **Taking it further**
>
> Using the Book Creator app, children can embed their character response videos into their written stories.

The role on the wall

"A film . . . should be a progression of moods and feelings." – Stanley Kubrick

We often ask pupils to write from the point of view of a character, including their emotions at certain points in the narrative. For this to take place effectively, it is important that children know how the character is feeling.

Taking it further

Use emojis to populate the character outline at various points in the narrative. Children will likely be familiar with different emojis and what they symbolise.

What makes us pick up a book time and again? Why is going to the cinema one of our most popular pastimes; and why is it that we can remember films that we last watched in our childhood? It is all about the emotion. The effect that the story has and how it makes us feel stays with us forever – when E.T. goes home, when we see the girl in the red coat in *Schindler's List* or when Artax succumbs to the swamp in *The Neverending Story*.

One tried-and-tested method of this is 'the role on the wall'. Give children an outline drawing of their character and ask them to record what the character is thinking in the head section of the diagram. Next, add how the character is feeling inside the body. Round the outside of the diagram, they should jot down what the other characters in the story think about the character in the spotlight. This activity can be completed at various points in the narrative to compare and contrast the children's different interpretations. This can then be used to scaffold independent writing. The activity could precede the Charting emotions activity (Idea 87).

Emojis in English

"I found emojis really useful when looking at emotions with my Year 1 class."

Children are familiar with emojis. They are widely used on social media; they are on wrapping paper; have been turned into cushions; and even used in requests for feedback by American presidential candidates. They can also be incredibly useful in the classroom.

The emoji has been used for years as a feedback method. They allow children to give their feedback in the form of a single emoji. Ask the children to critique their work or explain their understanding using emojis.

Children could easily create book reviews using only emojis. They could comment on characters and their opinions of chapters, etc. using the images to convey their ideas.

Give out emoji sheets along with emotion graphs (Idea 87) to help chart the change in emotions through a film clip used to stimulate writing. Watch how the character changes and ask the children to select the emoji which best represents their mood. These could then be elaborated with explanations as to what is making them feel this way.

Children could use emojis in visual planners for their work. These also work particularly well when story mapping or using a timeline mapper. Emojis can be used to make simple predictions in reading. During a guided reading lesson, ask the children what the character will do next or how the next chapter might end by providing emojis for the children to select from. Emojis are also a great way to give clues about the narrative. Select five or six emojis which could sum up the chapter, and ask the children to predict what happens.

Teaching tip

Prompts for writing could be given to the children in the form of emojis. Ask the children to interpret what could happen by giving them a selection of emojis to read.

Bonus idea ★

A fun way to introduce emojis is to ask the children to rewrite a story using emojis.

Break it down, build it up

"Rachel wore her green linen Easter suit she was so vain of, and her long whitish hair pulled off her forehead with a wide pink elastic hairband . . . " – Barbara Kingsolver, *The Poisonwood Bible*

Inspire children to describe a character or a creature by sharing an image with them to act as a stimulus and point of reference.

Teaching tip

Great images to inspire writing can be found on www.pobble365.com.

Begin by dividing the character or creature into its component parts, such as: eyes, mouth, nose, skin, hair, clothing, etc.

Designate these parts to groups of children who then work on creating a rich description of each component. This works particularly well when paired with vocabulary stations (Idea 6). The children could be provided with words and phrases on each table to use within their descriptive sentences.

There are various ways in which this can be brought together to create a complete description. Through shared writing, the teacher can create a model text by collating examples from pupils, taking care to select and edit to create an effective text. Alternatively, the descriptions can be displayed around the room, and children can select those that they like from each section to create a completed description.

Picture prompts can be sourced from a wide range of places. A brief internet search will provide hundreds of interesting images to use to engage the children. We like to supply a list of questions on the back of some images to stimulate the children's thinking:

- *Where is she going?*
- *Why does he have a scar?*
- *Where does it come from?*
- *How does it move?*

Building action sequences

"A good narrative action sequence can make or break a story."

A well-written action scene is fast-paced, hooks the reader in and captures the thrill of the moment. These are also one of the most difficult parts of narrative to write, though with a few tips, the children can succeed in constructing fabulous action sequences.

Create action chains by linking three to four pieces of action into a sequenced sentence:

He surged forwards with his foot on the ball, briefly looked up to align himself with the net, then pelted the ball with enough fury and energy to see it sail 50 yards and clatter home for 1:1 at half-time.

Use strong verbs and prepositions or adverbials of time to imply pace:

Just seconds later, he was hurtling down the left wing and darting away from their midfielder.

Encourage the children to use emotions and a range of sentence lengths to increase the pace and demonstrate the character's feelings:

Heart pounding, knee throbbing, he tore away from Number 8 and listened to the crowd. They were singing his song. Chants echoed in his ears and tears stung his eyes. He gathered momentum.

Keep dialogue short and punchy, or miss it out completely:

'Passssss!' he yelled at DeVictio.

Only use description to add to the tension or suspense:

The wound on his knee was stinging now, and a long ribbon of bright red blood was seeping down his sock towards his boot.

Encourage the use of figurative language to exaggerate and compare for effect:

He ran as though there were no tomorrow.

Bonus idea ★

Find action sequences in fiction writing and underline the key elements. Copy key words and save phrases to add to a 'borrowed board'.

Add an adventure

"Of course it is happening inside your head, Harry, but why on earth should that means that it is not real?" – J. K. Rowling, *Harry Potter and the Deathly Hallows*

Children have brilliant imaginations – just look at them in play. We can tap into that imagination in order to help them create fictional narratives.

Some children struggle to create their own narratives when they have to think about plotting events, character, setting and everything else that comes with writing.

When studying a narrative (film or text), children can write their own imaginative stories using the characters and settings that they become familiar with through deep reading.

Here are some examples:

When reading *Stig of the Dump* by Clive King, perhaps Stig and Barney find someone or something else in the quarry, such as a mammoth frozen in time.

In *The Graveyard Book* by Neil Gaiman, Nobody Owens meets a number of ghosts. Children could write about meeting a ghost of their own invention.

There is only one character in the animated short *Alma*. Children could add an extra character – the shopkeeper perhaps, or another child who warns Alma not to enter the shop.

In the books by Cressida Cowell, Hiccup and Toothless have many adventures. Children could emulate *How to Train Your Dragon* and create their own island for the heroes to visit and have new adventures on.

Paired writing tasks

"I was Red Riding Hood and Harley was the Wolf. Writing it together made us think about how our characters saw the situation."

Paired writing is a fabulous way to inject energy and enthusiasm into a piece of work.

First and foremost, pairings need to be precisely thought out. Children need to be paired with careful thought about ability. Additional support for some pairings needs to be considered, and expectations for some pairings may be different.

Ideas for paired writing:
- Children plan together. One child writes the opening and build-up, whilst the other writes the ending. The children then compose the dilemma and resolution together.
- Children compose a call-and-answer poem, as a piece of performance poetry.
- The children create diary entries about the same event, but as two different historical characters.
- The children create a dual narrative about an event from the perspective of the two characters. This works well when using a familiar text, e.g. Red Riding Hood and the wolf. I particularly like the piece to be written as one text.

  The woods were dark. I remembered mother's warning to stay to the paths and not to go where the trees tangled and light barely broke the canopy. *I saw her. She stood staring at the trees just a short distance from my feet. She held in her hands a basket and wore a sticky sweet smile which looked delicious.*
- Children could write a discussion text, putting forward two opposing views.

Walk and talk the story

"An author knows his landscape best; he can stand around, smell the wind, get a feel for his place." – Tony Hillerman

A rich description of setting can bring a piece of writing to life for the reader, so it is important that our young writers get it right.

Walking through their setting with friends allows them to imagine their setting in a physical space before verbalising it. During this verbalisation process, children can further enhance their imaginations through rich description, adding and editing passages to build an in-depth piece.

Start off by asking your children to brainstorm things that they may find in their settings. Ask them what they may see, hear, touch, smell, taste and feel in their setting. A soundtrack of sounds alongside some images may help to stimulate their imaginations.

Ask the children to record the things that they are imagining on a thought map, either individually or by collaborating in small groups.

Some children may need support and could choose from a given list of words and/or images.

Sort the children into groups, hand out rolls of paper around 2 m in length – wall paper backing is good for this – and ask children to draw a path through their landscape. Two lines in felt-tip pen will suffice. Next, ask the children in their group to think of the following:

- Five things that you see.
- Four things that you hear or smell.
- Three things you touch or feel.
- Two things you think you see.
- One feeling or emotion.

In their groups, the children negotiate these choices and write each one on a sticky note before adding it to their path. They then decide in what order they see or hear these things.

Once they have done the preparation work, they walk along the track, describing things as they go. One child may have added an 'old dead tree'. As their peer walks along the path, they may enhance this by saying 'an old dead tree with black skeletal branches'. They could add this with a sticky note.

When completed, the children can take a photograph of their map for their books, to help them write their setting description in their narrative.

This also works well when giving the children some time to search for their own images to add to the landscape. Sometimes, a child will have a very specific idea and will find it difficult to describe what they would like to see. Give the children 'search time' at the start of the lesson, so that they can add their own ideas to the pathway.

Taking it further

A further way to extend the lesson is to use the idea when on a school trip. This would not be possible in all scenarios, but could work well on a beach, at a farm or in the woods. Physically make the pathway using sticks, shells or by simply drawing into the sand. Give children time to record their 'five, four, three, two, one' and use stones to hold the paper down. Take pictures to use back in the classroom, or record the activity using a tablet.

Bonus idea

Children from other groups could visit the settings and be led through the path whilst the group narrates. This may give them additional ideas to add to their writing.

Developing dialogue with graphic novels

"When I was a boy, I always saw myself as a hero in comic books and movies. I grew up believing this dream." – Elvis Presley

Elvis loved comic books and movies, and so do many children. Teachers can use comics and graphic novels for a variety of reasons, including engaging reluctant readers.

Taking it further

Use a comic creator app such as Comic Life or Comics Head to create comic strips of original stories. There is also a comic strip creator program on www.readwritethink.org.

Graphic novels are a great scaffold to aid children with their narrative writing. It is easy to see what is being said, and who is saying it. When introducing inverted commas/speech marks, demonstrate that everything inside the speech bubble is written inside the inverted commas.

You can then model how to introduce the utterance, using the range of reporting clause structures. Each speaker in the graphic novel also has their own speech bubble. Demonstrate that when there is a new speaker and new bubble, a new line is started in their prose writing.

The initial rehearsal of the skill is done by rewriting the dialogue as prose. Teacher modelling is a vital part of showing how descriptions can be added between the sections of dialogue to move the narrative on.

To scaffold independent pieces of writing, photocopy pages of the novel with the speech bubbles blocked out in order for the children to add appropriate dialogue. Once this has been completed, the children can turn these into prose.

Writing about the weather

"Sunshine is delicious, rain is refreshing, wind braces us up, snow is exhilarating; there is really no such thing as bad weather, only different kinds of good weather." – John Ruskin

Describing the weather in stories adds an extra layer to the description of the setting. We all know that weather affects our moods, and in writing, the weather can affect the way we imagine a particular scene.

Sitting in a forest glade with a cool breeze on your back whilst the sun dapples through the leaves of the trees sounds idyllic to most people. If we were to just change the weather in the description, then the forest can sound like the last place any of us would want to be. Imagine standing in the forest glade, the branches offering scant shelter against the rain which streams relentlessly from the slate-grey sky, the wind biting at exposed flesh and chilling you to the bone. You are still in the same forest; the weather is doing all the work.

Simply describing the weather can establish when the narrative is taking place, e.g. if the sun is shining high in the sky overhead, the reader will know that the action is taking place in the afternoon.

Personification of weather is a device commonly used to add descriptive detail and help the reader create an image in their mind.

Some helpful examples of weather personified:

- *The sun smiled down happily.*
- *The mist slowly crawled through the trees, wrapping itself around each one.*
- *Rain attacked the faces of the commuters as they hurried towards the tube station.*

Taking it further

Develop descriptions of weather around a common theme, such as music, war or sounds.

Internal monologue

"I really enjoyed writing my internal monologue, pretending I was one of the Montgolfier brothers!"

Internal, or interior, monologue refers to the same thing: that stream of thoughts running through our minds. They can range in length from a line or two of thought to an in-depth insight into the frame of mind of the character.

First, and foremost, internal monologue should advance the action or build the character, so that it reveals something different from the bulk of the narrative.

They looked like a pack of wild dogs cornering their prey, as they stepped towards him, jeering and mocking his clothes.

I hate you; I hate you all so much.

Talk to the children about using reporting clauses. It is almost always entirely unnecessary to use reporting clauses like 'thought' or 'mused' as it should be apparent that the text is a line of internal monologue.

In longer sections of monologue, the reader is given the opportunity to connect more with the character. Emotions can be revealed, humour can be seen, the character's thoughts about other characters can become apparent.

- Children could create mini-monologues for characters in books they are studying.
- Use drama to explore a character's thoughts in a scene.
- Create monologues about a famous historical incident, e.g. Howard Carter finding Tutankhamun's tomb.
- Watch sections of film. Pause the film and ask the children to write mini-monologues from the point of view of one of the characters.

X factor sentences

"It was exciting to read my classmates' work and see which ones I thought had done a great job. Monty used an amazing adjective!"

Using the idea of selecting classwork which has the 'X factor' is a simple way for the children to make decisions about their own work, use criteria to critique the work of others and share work quickly with the whole class.

Begin by asking the children to select a section of their work which they would like to enter the X factor competition. To do this, the success criteria should be explicit. We often use the process for looking at individual sentences or short paragraphs; however, it would also work for phrases, clauses, descriptions, single stanzas of poetry, etc. – anything which would not be an onerous task to read in a short time. Once the children have selected their sentence, they write it onto their competition form. Next, they need to leave it on their table, or take it to a space, so that the whole class can move around and read it. Some children may need adult help. Give the children three stickers each (they could also be told to draw three ticks) which will be placed on the three most effective sentences. They need to meet the success criteria and they cannot select their own entires. At the end of the lesson, count how many stickers are on each piece of work. I often go around with stickers making sure that every piece of work has at least one sticker. The winner is the piece with the most stickers. Children might then win a small prize or go onto an X factor leader board.

Teaching tip

We usually use the plenary of the lesson to complete the X factor task, although there would also be some value in starting a lesson with the task, or in using it to check children's progress during a lesson.

Taking it further

Once children are experienced at using success criteria to make their selections, then they can begin to choose the writing that they find most effective.

Fairy tales reimagined

"If you want your children to be intelligent, read them fairy tales. If you want them to be more intelligent, read them more fairy tales." – Albert Einstein

Children are exposed to traditional tales from a very early age. This is true for many cultures and many countries. Children listen to the stories, read the books, watch the films and retell them with ease, and it is because of this love that writing new versions of fairy tales can have the most amazing outcomes.

Teaching tip

Collect and share a variety of alternative fairy tales such as: *The Three Ninja Pigs* by Corey Rosen Schwartz; *The Three Little Aliens and the Big Bad Robot* by Margaret McNamara; *Previously* by Allan Ahlberg; and *Jack and the Baked Beanstalk* by Colin Stimpson.

1) Introduce a new character. Consider whether this will be a protagonist or antagonist and how they will advance the story.
2) Switch the roles of the hero/heroine and the villain. Write it from the point of view of one of the characters.
   Switch the characters of the Big Bad Wolf and Red Riding Hood. Tell the story from the wolf's point of view.
3) Switch settings with another fairy tale. Could the *Three Little Pigs* be set in the city?
4) Create a hybrid fairy tale. Try mixing two different stories and get the children to consider where they might converge. Could the characters cross over?
5) Write a prequel or a sequel. This might also involve introducing new characters, or perhaps using the idea of a hybrid text.
6) Introduce a new quest for the characters. Perhaps Red Riding Hood has more wolves to kill once the news of her success spreads?
7) Put yourself in the fairy tale. This idea can work fabulously well with younger children. Maybe the Big Bad Wolf starts school in your class!

8) Modernise the story. Bring it up to date with a retelling that features today's technology, clothes, trends and crazes.
9) Re-tell the story in a different genre. Try writing the story as a newspaper article, poem or recount it from the point of view of one of the characters.
10) Challenge the children to include a set list of objects in their retelling. This can completely change the story, depending upon the criteria given to the children.

Bonus idea ★

Collect a variety of modern retellings of classic fairy tales, such as *Ever Clever Eva* by Andrew Fusek Peters or *Beowulf the Brave* by Julia Green, for the school library. Use these to spark initial interest in this idea.

Writing historical narratives

"One of the absolute joys of teaching is to create historical narratives with the children."

Children enjoy the process of using the knowledge and understanding gained through a thematic approach or topic work to create narrative pieces.

Character

The children should already have some knowledge of the characters likely to appear in their narrative. Hints within their writing, e.g. about the clothing, and clues about how the characters live are incredibly important. A poor child living in Victorian London would dress, live and behave differently to a wealthy child of that time.

Dialogue

For real authenticity, ensure that the children have considered how their character would speak. Discuss words and phrases which would be used at the time, but remind the children not to fill the narrative with so much that the dialogue becomes difficult to understand. Play clips to the children, so that they can hear how speech would have sounded.

Setting

This is an integral part of the writing. The children should already have some idea of what life was like during the time chosen. Information needs to be accurate. The children should have considered what the landscape was like, what everyday items would have been used, what buildings were like, the interior of houses and what people ate. That is why writing a historical narrative at the end of a themed unit will ensure the children have far more success.

Plot

The plot should reflect what would be appropriate for the time. If the children are featuring famous historical characters, then they will need to have prior knowledge about them and the event they are writing about.

How to support the children in the narrative process

Provide them with word banks to use during their narrative writing. Leave some boxes blank, so that the children can look back through topic work, etc. and add to the word bank themselves. Ensure word banks are discussed and that the children understand how to use the vocabulary given in them.

Provide opportunities for drama work to precede writing. Develop characters through hot seating (Idea 54) and internal monologues (Idea 64). Get children to consider body language and mannerisms. Write interviews with the main character and use the 'role on the wall' technique (Idea 55) to consider the character's views, opinions and feelings alongside their characteristics and external appearance.

Children should write short descriptions of settings and characters prior to creating their narrative, so that they can include some of the information in their longer piece.

A great technique is to write a 'the day before' narrative. Ask the children to consider the point at which they will begin their narrative and (two or three days before writing the piece) develop a shorter piece entitled, *The Day Before*. Children will have seen this technique used in film, where we learn about the characters' movements the day before during a short flashback. They can then use the piece to begin to build the world that the character lives in. There does not need to be any major event or dilemma; rather the children should see it as a setting of the scene.

Bonus idea ★

Examine images of the time being studied. Look at how rich and poor dressed and how men and women dressed; look at buildings and note down features the children might need to consider when writing. Provide photographs, art and film clips, if possible.

Writing prequels

"Prequels should provide nods to the original, and yet have an exciting story of their own."

Writing a prequel can be a clever way to develop a back story to an original text. Characters can often leave question marks in our minds as readers; therefore a prequel is a fabulous way to encourage the children to really consider what happened before the original text.

Teaching tip

A really effective way of giving the children a stimulus to write from is to provide them with a film clip as their original stimulus. Clips are a faster way of learning the story and then the writing process can begin more quickly. For a wide range of clips use www.literacyshed.com.

To write their prequel, the children must have a solid understanding of the original story. It is always a good idea to track a story timeline on paper so that the children remember what happened and when. Next, it is extremely important that the children have enough facts about the characters who will feature in their prequel. It is actually far easier to feature a secondary character in the prequel than to base it around a primary or main character. After this, it is essential that the children decide upon the timeframe their story will cover, and at which point, if at all, it catches up with the original.

Top tips for the children

- A prequel often reveals something about the character, or a secret about the plotline of the original, so think about WHAT your story will be about.
- The story should READ like the original; therefore, there is no problem with using *some* words and phrases which are written by the original author.
- Look for clues in the original text to weave into the prequel.
- Add twists which don't directly change the original, but which make the reader think, 'A-ha!'.
- Grow the character — develop their story so that it moves in the direction of the original.

Bonus idea ★

Ask the children to write the prequel from a different or unusual perspective.

Epic endings

"I used to just write, 'The End' but now I try to really choose an ending that keeps my readers hooked until the last word."

All too often, young writers put their heart and soul into creative and engaging narrative writing, only for it to fall at the last hurdle: the ending. However, by teaching a range of narrative endings, the children can decide how best to round off their work and how to keep the reader interested.

Question: This leaves the reader to ponder upon the question and can also be a good way to imply that there is more to the story. It can pave the way for a sequel.

Moral: The main character learns something through the course of the narrative and often reflects upon the outcomes of their changes.

Twist: Encourage the children not to go too far with their twists. A twist ending should leave the reader feeling as though they were surprised by the ending, not that it was unrealistic or over the top.

Emotional: These do not need to necessarily end in a positive way. I remember reading *Private Peaceful* with a class of Year 6 children and sobbing our way through the last paragraphs. Yet that book was absolutely adored by those children, who all agreed it was the perfect ending.

Back to the start: This is sometimes known as a circular ending. Often lines and words are repeated and the reader gains an understanding of why events unfolded as they did.

Hint about the future: These endings 'fast forward' to a point in time where the reader gains insight into the future life of the characters.

Solution: One of the most commonly-used endings features the main character finding a solution to the problem in the story.

Teaching tip

When you come across endings that fit in with the definitions here, photocopy them and display them in class as models.

Shifts in formality

"Guided reading is a great opportunity to look for shifts in formality."

For a child to be judged as 'working at greater depth' in KS2, the child needs to demonstrate that they can manage shifts in formality within their writing – the key word being 'manage'.

The teaching of this skill, and how to achieve this within writing, is not something that should be solely kept for the Year 6 classroom. In fact, all children need to experience this, so that they can start to identify it when reading and refine the skill themselves, to the point where they can 'manage' it. There are a number of genres or devices which lend themselves well to making shifts in formality.

Journalistic writing – The difference in tone between the majority of the piece and the direct quotes from those involved in the story. *'I was shocked! It was ginormous!' stated Mr Li.*

Diary writing – Parentheses can allow the writer to change the formality within the piece. *She stood and smiled at me (it was a big, fat grin if I'm being honest) and I stared back at her.*

Persuasive writing – The tone in which the piece is written may slip to a more informal tone in order to connect with the reader.

Letter writing – These may use an informal tone, in parts, when showing a more light-hearted approach to subject matter. *We will aim to be there at around midday – though Dad is driving, so it could take a week!*

Narrative writing – Dialogue can be a way to show a difference in formality, as well as first-person narration. *'You and whose army?' she yelled.*

Rhetorical questions – These can be a useful tool for slipping into a more informal tone, and can be used in both fiction and non-fiction writing. *Was he for real?*

Summary headlines

"SUPER CALEY GO BALLISTIC CELTIC ARE ATROCIOUS!"

Being able to condense a whole narrative into a single line is a skill that will allow pupils to play with language and show that they have understood that which they have read.

Newspaper headline writers use a range of features which you could introduce to the children in order for them to create their own:

- Alliteration
- Rhyme
- Word play
- Short and snappy
- Often humorous, but can be serious too.

Borrow some headlines from the world of sport to demonstrate the features of headlines. If a football team signed a new goalkeeper from Russia, the headline might read: FROM RUSSIA WITH GLOVES, which is a play on the James Bond title.

FAIRYTALE FINISH FOR FREDDIE FLINTOFF is a great example of alliteration.

One of the most famous sporting headlines of all time came after a match when Inverness Caledonian Thistle (Caley) won the cup 3–1 against Celtic. It read, 'SUPER CALEY GO BALLISTIC CELTIC ARE ATROCIOUS' playing on the famous song from *Mary Poppins*.

Children could have a go at creating their own headlines for their favourite books.

BIG BAD WOLF GETS BOILED BOTTOM – *The Three Little Pigs*

ROBBIN' RICH IS RIGHT FOR ROBIN – *Robin Hood*

Teaching tip

To engage pupils who are reluctant to read, use short films to inspire headlines, or try using familiar traditional tales.

Creating content for non-fiction writing

"It was easier because I didn't have to worry about getting all the facts and figures wrong. I just made them up."

What matters most when writing in an English lesson? As English teachers, we need to balance on that fine line between accurate reporting of facts and writing which includes effective use of language and grammatical structures.

When writing non-fiction, children have to be able to recall facts and then present them effectively. Novice writers, who may lack sufficient knowledge, in terms of content or writing experience, may find combining the two difficult. To make it simpler, focus in English lessons on the writing element, rather than the content.

You could give out information sheets which the children could use in their writing. However, then there is a danger of them creating a facsimile of what they have been presented with, rather than an individual piece of writing.

Instead of giving children all the information that they need, allow them to create their own. This gives them the freedom to be creative: to focus on the writing process and to become the experts on the content.

Recount/review a school trip to a theme park. Children make the decisions about the name of the rides, how fast they travel, admission costs and other facilities available.

Explain how to look after a fantasy creature. Children can choose what their creature looks like, its diet, its habitat and how best to exercise it.

Instructions for a new invention. It does not matter which order the instructions come in, so children can focus on the language of instruction.

Bonus idea ★

Have a class debate, and use the debate to formulate non-fiction writing in terms of persuasion and discussion.

Writing instructions from fictional stimuli

"I like writing about things that I know about. It just comes out easier."

As context makes learning memorable, use the current class book as a stimulus for instructional writing.

Tap into pupils' prior knowledge of stories in order to create a set of instructions for a specific character using genre-specific language.

Start with simple instructive sentences which they can analyse with the pupils, in order to demonstrate the imperative nature of them, e.g. 'Walk slowly into the woods.'

Walk – imperative verb tells you *what* to do.

Slowly – adverb of manner tells you *how* to do it.

Into the woods – prepositional phrase tells you *where* to do it.

Neil Gaiman's book *Instructions* demonstrates how this can be done effectively in order to walk a character through a story.

'Touch the wooden gate in the wall you never saw before. Say "please" before you open the latch, go through, walk down the path.'

If children know the story of *Goldilocks*, then they will able to adapt this to create a set of instructions, e.g. *'Leave your house in the morning. Walk down the path. When you come to a cottage, go in. Sit on a chair'*.

Teaching tip

Ask children to create word bank displays by sharing their adverbs of manner and imperative verbs on sticky notes on English working walls.

Taking it further

Once the children get the hang of instructions, ask them to include other features such as modality: 'If the porridge is too hot, then try another'.

Film for research

"I feel like an expert now!"

Asking children to research a topic can often be fraught with obstacles. If there is a lack of suitable texts in the school library on a given subject (or even a lack of library facilities) or insufficient ICT provision to use the internet for research, consider using a film instead.

Teaching tip

This activity is a perfect opportunity to use graphic organiser software such as www.popplet.com.

There are additional problems with traditional research methods in the primary school. Children will sometimes copy down vast swathes of information which they do not comprehend.

The key skills of note making include selecting key information and organising it in a succinct, accessible and memorable way. You can develop these skills in the children by using films to generate the information.

The benefits of using film in this way:

- All children can access the same information.
- Reluctant/slow readers will access the information at the same speed as their peers.
- Pupils will have to summarise the spoken words in their own words, rather than copy from the text.

Prior to note making, it is important that the teacher demonstrates different ways of making notes, so that the children can choose how they would like to do it. They may like to use bullet points, mind maps, pictorial representations, or a mixture of these.

Some interesting sources for non-fiction films:

The Literacy Shed – www.literacyshed.com
Bear Grylls' *Born Survivor*
BBC Newsround – www.bbc.co.uk/newsround
First News Today – www.live.firstnews.co.uk
National Geographic Kids – www.natgeokids.com

Inspiring explanation texts

"I found that using a film clip hooked the children from the start – they were bursting to write."

An explanation text is a piece of writing which explains how or why something happens or works. Explanation texts rely heavily upon the children's previous knowledge of a subject, to be able to write with any level of expertise on the matter, which is fabulous when using a thematic approach to the curriculum. Therefore, I often turn to film clips or fiction writing as a stimulus for explanatory writing.

This does not mean to say that there should be a cessation of writing explanatory texts based upon learning in topic. However, film clips, because of their brevity, often allow us to learn a great deal in a short amount of time. Children could watch non-fiction clips which explain a process. Allow the children to make notes, on their first watching, of the sequence of events. During the second viewing, they should note down technical vocabulary and consider the presentational features they want to use. I have often found that some of the most successful writing has come from topics which the children have no prior knowledge of, e.g. the migration of the Christmas Island crabs, or how the zombie snail parasite invades its host.

I also use fiction clips to inspire explanation writing. Children derive deep joy from creating their own 'hexapod' based upon the film, *Avatar*, and 'documentary' about the fictional moon, Pandora. Once the children have created a hexapod, they can create their own explanatory texts about how it feeds or how it hunts. The same is true for explaining how to play Quidditch (don't confuse this with writing instructions) or explaining how the machine in *Cloudy with a Chance of Meatballs* creates the food.

Bonus idea ★

Using fiction writing, such as explaining how the potion turns Jekyll into Hyde or explaining how frobscottle creates whizzpoppers in *The BFG*, ensures that the children do not need to have any prior knowledge of the subject.

Figurative language

"She mastered figurative language as easily as a knife cuts through butter."

Figurative language can engage the reader by using non-literal descriptions. Here are some ideas for how to teach various types.

Simile/metaphor
With younger children, introduce similes through 'friend poetry'. Ask the children to devise a poem which uses different similes, for different friends.

James runs as fast as a cheetah; Heidi's smile is bright as sunshine.

For older children, play a range of familiar songs and ask them to listen for the simile or metaphor. All lyrics should be checked beforehand.

Hyperbole/exaggeration
Distribute sentence openings, and ask the children to finish off as either an exaggeration or hyperbole.

My mum made a stack of pancakes that you could see from the moon.

Alliteration
Ask the children to complete the menu for an Alliteration Animal X Factor:

Amazing Acrobatic Armadillos; Brilliant Balancing Baboons.

Personification
Provide a pile of nouns to be personified and, in another pile, verbs to use in a personification. Allow the children to select three verbs each time. If they can create a personification using the noun and the first verb, then they get 20 points. If they must use the second verb, they get ten points; and if they must select the third verb, they get five points.

Welsh train stations

"They were on the lip of a circular hollow in the side of the mountain. This was filled with a blue flower, a rock plant of some sort . . . "
– W. Golding, *Lord of the Flies*

Above we can see how Golding constructs his descriptions in *Lord of the Flies*; he leads us stumbling through the scene by adding more and more details, linked with prepositional phrases. We can encourage the children to do this in an engaging way.

Llanfairpwllgwyngyllgogerychwyrndrobwllllant ysiliogogogoch is the longest place name in Europe. Translated into English, this place name is quite descriptive and uses prepositional language: 'St Mary's Church in the hollow of the white hazel near to the rapid whirlpool of Llantysilio of the red cave'.

With the children, discuss how adjectives have been used for description in the example, and how prepositional adverbs are used to extend the sentence. Ask children to create their own Welsh station name in order to write a description of an object or character. Choose an appropriate image.

The sentence may be lengthened like this:

The tree is in the field.

The tree with the long branches is in the field.

The tree with the long branches is in the field surrounded by long grass beneath the star-filled sky.

Even more description could be added by adding adverbs and adjectives and inserting it into a narrative piece.

The dead tree with the long whip-like branches stood forlornly in the foreign field, surrounded by the long, green grass beneath the black, star-filled sky.

> **Bonus idea** ★
>
> Use Google Translate to roughly translate their English-language place name into Welsh to see who can create the longest place name.

Poetry

Part 5

Encouraging a poetry-rich environment

"I have never started a poem yet whose end I knew. Writing a poem is discovering." – Robert Frost

So, what can we do to ensure that our learning environments help to foster a love and understanding of poetry?

- Have poetry visible around the school.
- Invite poets into school and involve all children.
- Introduce a poet of the month and use this across the school and in assemblies.
- Make sure the children have access to a broad variety of poetry at all times. Poetry shouldn't only be available during the poetry unit you are teaching.
- Use poetry in other areas of the curriculum. We once found out an incredible amount of information about WW1 simply by reading poems in a history lesson.
- Look at the English curriculum in your school; is there enough poetry being taught?
- Make sure children perform their own pieces, and learned texts, to different audiences.
- Encourage parents, teachers and other pupils to recommend poems they love.
- Develop teachers' knowledge of poetry and ensure the children are accessing texts from a variety of cultures, styles and times.
- Be creative when teaching poetry – provide clues, visual stimuli and performances to spark children's interest before starting to read.
- Look at poems which follow rules and those which break rules. Look at 'conventional' examples and things like slam poetry and rap.
- Encourage children's response to poetry in a variety of different forms.
- Collect language and explore how it fits (or doesn't) together.

Writing short poems

"I loved writing my animal cinquain because I thought very hard about exactly the right words to use."

The restrictions applied to writing haikus and cinquains make them appealing to children and can be quite challenging, so it is essential that they have time to play with the language and to re-draft.

Haikus and cinquains are similar in nature because of the restrictions used to produce them. A haiku is a poem from Japan that consists of 17 syllables in three, or fewer, lines. The most familiar pattern of these syllables is to use five on the first line, seven on the second and five on the third. They do not need to rhyme, though to challenge the children you could ask them to rhyme lines one and three:

Cat curls on my lap,
Purring and twitching her nose,
Then resumes her nap.

A cinquain is similar as it uses a constraint, though, in the case of the cinquain, this is based upon words and not syllables. The cinquain uses five lines and uses the pattern: one, two, three, four, one (words) as the skeleton for the writing. When first introducing the cinquain to the children, a 'recipe' for cinquain writing is useful:

Line 1 – Think of a noun. (cat)
Line 2 – Use two adjectives to describe the noun. (stealthy, agile)
Line 3 – Use three verbs linked to the noun. (prowling, stalking, catching)
Line 4 – Use four words to describe the noun. (slinking in the shadows)
Line 5 – Repeat the noun. (cat)

Teaching tip

Children really enjoy the challenge of this form of poetry. It is also useful to give out a variety of haikus and cinqains and ask the children to spot the imposter.

Taking it further

Try introducing tankas to the children. These are based upon five lines and use the pattern five, seven, five, seven, seven syllables.

91

Found poems

"I teach it as though the poems are already there, just waiting to be found."

Found poems, sometimes known as blackout poetry, use a wide range of texts as a medium through which to search for words and phrases. Found poems are often thought of as a collage of language.

Method 1

Distribute to the children sections of narrative text which feature a theme to be the basis for the found poem. In the past, I have had great success with war poetry, using texts such as *Private Peaceful* by Michael Morpurgo. I have also seen some amazing work produced by using *Strange Case of Dr Jekyll and Mr Hyde* and the description of his transformation. Ask the children to work through the page or pages and look for words and phrases which stand out. Circle these in pencil. Keep moving through the narrative until a list of words and phrases begin to appear, and then begin to piece them together as a poem. By using the blackout method, the writer selects which parts of the book to blackout and leaves their chosen words and phrases visible for the reader to see. Though there is also a lot to be said for taking the words out of the book and re-ordering them to produce the poem.

Method 2

Use a wider range of media, e.g. magazine articles, newspapers, leaflets, etc. The children should trawl through the texts looking for headlines, sub-headings, words and phrases they'd like to borrow. These can then be cut directly from the source or written onto a separate sheet. We have found success with using large sheets of sugar paper and getting the children to repeat some words and phrases they find, almost like verse and chorus.

Spine poems

"We walked through the library like poetry detectives!"

The spine poem is another kind of found poem, though this takes a larger number of books and the time to sit and play around with the language.

The idea of the spine poem is that the writer uses the titles of other books to become the lines in each stanza of their poem. It is often helpful to start with a theme, such as animals. Take the children to the school library if possible, or provide them with a wide range of books per table. To begin, the children might work on a single-stanza poem. As the children become more confident, they may decide to play around more with the language, attempting rhymes or using repetition. The children should make a note of any titles which they think would fit together. It is useful to ask the children to pile the books on top of one another, so that the poem becomes instantly visible when looking at the spines. These could then be documented through photography. It is useful to begin with four-line poems, as these are fairly straightforward for most children. The children need to peruse the titles until they find four which fit together as a poem. This is where you could encourage repetitions, etc. for a second stanza:

> Lost at the zoo,
> The enormous crocodile,
> Please don't eat me!
> Crocodile tea!
>
> Lost at the zoo,
> Don't laugh at giraffe,
> Giraffes can't dance,
> Oh dear, Geoffrey!

Teaching tip

It is sometimes useful to allow children to look up, using a tablet, a book to fit the theme of their poem.

Performance poetry

"The children fell in love with the poem and brought me to tears as they performed it."

With the National Curriculum's requirement for the children to 'build up a repertoire' of learned poems, performance poetry is an ideal way to engage the children with the text.

Taking it further

Film the class performing their poem at different points. Use it to help them evaluate and critique themselves.

Children love a poem with humour, so poems like 'Gran, can you rap?' by Jack Ousby are fabulous for appealing to children. However, some of the most powerful performances I have seen have come from the recital of war poetry and Shakespearean quotes.

Whichever poem you select, it is essential that the children explore the following:

- Pace
- Pauses
- Punctuation
- Pitch
- Repetition
- Layering
- Emphasis
- Volume
- Body language
- Movement

- To begin, ensure the children understand all vocabulary. They will be unable to connect with a poem which they do not understand.
- Look at literal and inferred meanings to the poem and discuss the tone – who is saying the poem? What is the theme? Do the children need to imagine a character? Move on to look at the way that the poem has been structured. What are the stanzas about? Are there repetitions? Does it build to a certain point?
- Finally, look at how to perform it. Develop ideas about the pace of the piece. Does the punctuation help you to understand pauses and stops? Would elements work with more than one voice? Which words need more emphasis? How might volume be important?
- Ask the children to consider their body language as they perform.

Teaching tip

Play vocal and facial warm-ups before asking the children to begin any performance work.

Using ballads for narrative writing

"The mirror crack'd from side to side, 'The curse is come upon me!' cried the Lady of Shalott." – Alfred, Lord Tennyson

Ballads make an excellent stimulus for narrative writing because of their detailed nature and the messages they often contain.

These lengthy poems often have a musical quality because of their rhyming pattern. Some interesting ballads to share with children include 'The Raven' by Edgar Allan Poe, 'The Rime of the Ancient Mariner' by Samuel Taylor Coleridge and 'The Lady of Shalott' by Alfred, Lord Tennyson.

In a similar format to that of the narrative poem, introduce the poem by giving children clues to the story. In the case of 'The Lady of Shalott', ask the children to piece together the story by showing them the John William Waterhouse paintings. Complete sequencing activities and language development before reading the poem. Explore the poem by looking at the descriptions it offers, and produce story maps of what happens in the narrative. Ask the children to re-tell the story orally. Complete 'language lifter' activities where the children 'sieve' the text for examples of language to use within their own narrative. Explore the figurative language used and imagery created in the poem. Use drama to explore the scenes, characters and emotions in the piece. Produce descriptions of the setting and the characters based upon the information in the poem. Write sections of dialogue between characters. Use non-fiction writing to explore the story further, e.g. newspaper reports and interviews with the characters. Build up towards creating a piece of narrative based upon the story told in the poem.

Teaching tip

With longer ballads, an interesting method to try is to ask the children to base their story around a particular stanza or stanzas.

Narrative poetry as a non-fiction stimulus

"The children loved using clues to piece together the story behind the poem."

Poetry can elicit an amazing response from the children and can be used as a wonderful non-fiction stimulus.

Teaching tip

Provide the children with a version of the text broken into separate stanzas. Don't do this with very long pieces. Ask the children to read and to place into the order in which they believe the poem was written.

There are a number of narrative poems that are suitable for primary-aged children, although some language choices may need to be discussed with the class. Here are some of our favourites:

- 'The Highwayman' – Alfred Noyes
- 'The Jumblies' – Edward Lear
- 'The Listeners' – Walter de la Mare
- 'The Tay Bridge Disaster' – William McGonagall

Introduce the poem by giving out clues and a pre-prepared glossary so that the children can look up vocabulary, such as 'breeches' or 'girders'. Give the children about a week to familiarise themselves with the 'facts' of the poem before attempting to use the text as a basis for their non-fiction writing. Some ideas for non-fiction responses:

- Letters
- Diaries/journals/logs
- Persuasive texts
- Discursive texts
- Biographical/autobiographical writing
- Newspaper articles/journalistic writing
- First-person recounts of the events
- Instructions/manuals/guides.

Some examples of these might be to write a series of letters between the fated lovers in 'The Highwayman'. 'The Tay Bridge Disaster' lends itself well to journalistic writing, or the children could create a piece of persuasive writing from the point of view of the Jumblies, explaining the merits of going to sea in a sieve.

Nonsense poetry for grammar lessons

"Where the Cows go Bong!" – Spike Milligan, 'On the Ning Nang Nong'

If children understand the grammar rules that they have been taught, then they should be able to demonstrate this with any text. This can be explained to the children with the aid of nonsense poems.

When developing grammar skills, unfamiliar language can become a burdensome stumbling block. However, children need to be able to apply their knowledge to a range of texts.

Take this extract from 'The Jabberwocky' in Lewis Carroll's *Alice's Adventures in Wonderland*.

> 'He took his vorpal sword in hand:
> Long time the manxome foe he sought –
> So rested he by the Tumtum tree,
> And stood a while in thought.
>
> And, as in uffish thought he stood,
> The Jabberwock, with eyes of flame,
> Came whiffling though the tulgey wood,
> And burbled as it came!'

In the first stanza, we come across some unfamiliar adjectives – 'vorpal' and 'manxome'. We know that they are adjectives because they immediately precede a noun.

In the second stanza, the reader is presented with two unfamiliar verbs – 'whiffling' and 'burbled'. We can identify 'whiffling' as a verb due to its context – the fact that he is doing it through the woods and because it has the regular present tense verb suffix '–ing'. In the last line, the Jabberwock 'burbled' as he came. Again, we know the context and positioning of the word in the sentence and the suffix '–ed' indicates a regular past tense verb.

Taking it further

Children could create dictionary definitions for the nonsense words.

97

Using film and image

Part 6

Adding dialogue to films

"Because we had seen the characters speaking, it was easy to decide what they would be saying in the next scene."

When we watch films, we observe and follow characters speaking together. This speech often moves the action forwards and reveals how the characters are feeling and what they are thinking. Because they are often familiar with the way in which films work, children can analyse what the characters say and predict what they will say next.

Whilst using a film for stimulus, choose a scene to watch without any sound. Ask the children to discuss what they think is being said. They may draw upon the body language of the characters to form their opinion, or it may be due to the context of the conversation, i.e. the setting or the events in the previous scene.

This activity can also be carried out using films which have no dialogue in them. The children's interpretation of body language, character, setting and events will allow them to form ideas about what is being said. In the music video *Titanium* by David Guetta, we see a worried teacher talking to a police officer as a young boy cycles away. Children are able to create credible dialogue for this section of the video.

Children can also be creative and change the direction of the narrative by altering what a character says. In *Titanium*, for example, the teacher could say to the police officer a number of things:

> *'He is the only one who survived!' said the teacher pointing at the young boy with a worried look.*

This would be very different to:

> *'He is the one who committed the heinous crime!' whispered the teacher with a look of terror.*

Charting emotions – put yourself in their shoes

"Once I had completed my chart, I knew exactly what to write about and what order I needed to write it in."

There are a number of writing opportunities across the primary curriculum which require the children to write empathetically, putting themselves 'in the shoes' of a character in first-person narratives, diary writing and in fictional recounts. It is therefore important that children realise how a character is feeling at each key point of the narrative.

Once the children understand how the character feels at each point, they can chart them on a line graph so that they can add further details to inform their writing. It is important to add at this point that some children may need additional support when it comes to recognising emotions.

Provide the children with a blank graph. Label the Y axis in two parts – **positive** and **negative** – and along the X axis, place the key points of the narrative: between six and eight should be sufficient. Children then plot how the character was feeling at each point, comparing with the other events and deciding why some events are more positive than others.

Once each point has been plotted, a key word to describe the feeling at each point can be added. Children should be adventurous in their choices rather than choosing ordinary words such as 'happy' or 'sad'. See also ideas for using emojis in English (Idea 56).

The character's main thought could also be added at each point too. This chart then leads the writer through their narrative.

Teaching tip

To extend the activity, add a second character with contrasting feelings and plot them onto the same graph in a different colour.

Film as a narrative scaffold

"Films are just stories brought to life."

If you ask children to tell you a story, then they will often draw upon their own experiences of storytelling. This may be from oral retellings at bedtime, from stories that they have read themselves, or from the stories they have seen on screen. Observe children at play and you will see even the youngest taking roles of characters from shows that they enjoy and recreating these stories or adding new adventures.

Teaching tip

Showing a film in its entirety can sometimes be essential for teaching, though there may be times when it would be more appropriate to show different elements of a clip at different stages, or in a different order.

Film and animation can be used to scaffold the storytelling process in a more formal manner too. Firstly, choose a short film or animation, such as those found on www.literacyshed.com (although this activity can be done with any film or extract). Then break the film down into scenes; this can be done in collaboration with the children. Watch the film back and discuss the role of each scene within the whole.

Some examples may be:

- To introduce a setting
- To show how a character is feeling
- To develop a problem for the character
- To introduce the villain
- To transition between two locations.

Discuss how the director is successful in achieving the desired effect, and how this could be achieved through writing.

The main points of the story can then be emulated by the children in order to create their own retellings, or as an adaptable framework to create their own narrative.

The key points can be presented as a list, or through a flow chart of images that children can follow and apply their own vocabulary and structures to.

Scene by scene into sentences

"Everything I learned, I learned from the movies." – Audrey Hepburn

It is true that, as well as being inspiring stimuli, films can also be used to scaffold plot and writing techniques.

Films can be broken down into shots and scenes – their writing counterparts being sentences and paragraphs.

In the short animation, *DreamGiver*, by Ty Carter (see www.vimeo.com/36833415), there are seven key scenes:

- Setting introduction
- Character introduction
- A secret is revealed
- A problem occurs
- A new setting is introduced
- The problem gets worse
- The problem is resolved.

1. Show the children a number of film settings to demonstrate common features of setting introduction, such as zooming in, panning, use of colour and sounds, etc., all of which can be signposted by you and emulated by the children.

2. Bullet-point the information and events in the scene. This could be done with sticky notes on tables or as a class activity. Note down key words which could be used. Use contextualised grammar teaching to consider adjectives which fit within the scene.

3. Now begin to formulate sentences. Spend time teaching 'show, don't tell' sentences and a range of openers. Focus on figurative language, and model sentences for the children to see the writing process in action.

Teaching tip

Return to the film repeatedly throughout the lesson to look at how the director wants the viewer to see the scene. In writing, look at sentence lengths and how these impact upon the reader.

Taking it further

Once sentences have been constructed, begin to look at how to move towards paragraphing.

Replicating camera angles in narrative writing

"I didn't know filming a movie was so complicated. Everything we see has to be decided by someone for a reason."

In addition to mise-en-scène, the camera angles used in film making are carefully chosen for a variety of effects. These can be a little trickier to analyse, as can the shot type and the reason why the director has chosen a particular angle. However, as writers, children can use this information to enhance their narrative.

Here are some of the simpler shot types that the children can imitate in their writing.

The establishing shot
Usually, the first shot of a new scene, this shot shows the audience where the action is taking place.
In writing: Start a new paragraph with an establishing phrase, usually an adverb or preposition of place, to show the reader where the action is, e.g. *in the dusty attic; behind the school; at the fairground.*

The long shot
Usually, the long shot shows the character at full length and places them in their surroundings.
In writing: This can be copied by describing where the character is, once the setting has been established, e.g. if the setting is the fairground, then the 'long shot' may describe the main character queuing for tickets or entering the gates with their friends.

The mid shot
This general-purpose shot can be used to display a character's body language or to show the head and shoulders of characters involved in dialogue.
In writing: This could be the signal for description of a character, or the point at which to introduce some dialogue.

Close-up or extreme close-up

These shots occur in order to pick up small details on a character's face. They lead to a feeling of intimacy and connection between the character and the audience, whilst conveying mood or emotion.

In writing: Close-ups encourage children to add details about a character's feelings by choosing a particular aspect of their movements to describe. The writer may describe nervous fingers tapping on a desk, a lip being chewed by someone in deep contemplation, or the knitted brows of a character about to go into battle.

The panning shot

This simple shot takes in more of the scene with a movement of the camera from left to right (or right to left) or up and down (vertical panning shot).

In writing: The children could create a top-to-toe description of their character in the style of a vertical shot. They might describe a building from the ground up, or perhaps create a horizontal panning shot by describing a scene from left to right. In action, the panning shot follows the action or points the reader in the direction that the action is moving.

The whip pan

This is where the pan happens so fast that the picture blurs so that the image is mostly unrecognisable. It is often accompanied by a sound to indicate the speed at which something has happened. The image then refocuses.

In writing: In an action sequence, the movement between two points could be written as a whip pan. The child would need to build up the tension/suspense and then indicate a sudden change in events. This could be through onomatopoeia, or a suitable conjunction:

His feet thundered on the ground as he ran towards the treeline, with the torches and shouts getting closer behind him. WHOOSH! A net, hidden beneath leaves and debris, scooped him up and suspended him above the forest floor.

Taking it further

Look at other shots and camera angles and ask the children to suggest ways in which they could feature these as writing.

Zooming in and out

"I like to pretend I have got a telescope and that I am describing what I can see through it!"

The zooming in (and out) technique is often seen in films. The director will select what is best to focus on and then zoom in and out accordingly, depending upon what they want the viewer to see. This can also be an incredibly effective way of writing.

We will talk about zooming in, as zooming out is simply the reverse process. Imagine a scene in a film where a key element is revealed or highlighted. The wider scene changes to magnify details in one area of specific interest. The writer will aim to include the following:

- A magnified key point of interest
- Use of 'show, don't tell' technique
- Building of tension
- Very small details
- Emotions and reactions from the characters to give clues.

To introduce the idea to the children, give out images which feature some element of surprise or interest. The children need to begin by setting up their 'establishing shot' by describing the entire scene, in context, briefly:

She looked up at number 544 and sighed. This was it. Not extraordinary in any way. A dull, grey building – probably built in the 1920s – with sad, peeling paint and a dejected-looking front porch. There was a narrow alleyway which ran around the side of the property, and a tired-looking garden, though most of the plants were wildly overgrown or had died long ago.

A good tip is to feature a single line which acts as a zoom into the close-up:

And then she saw it . . .

Encourage the children to slowly reveal their 'close-up'. Imagine that the camera pans slowly up to the point of interest. The children should add even the smallest of details to make the writing more 'real'. Look at building 'show, not tell' sentences, so that the reader is using the clues to infer and deduce information about the scene:

Through the overgrown grass and weeds, a broken path led up the centre of the garden, towards the house, just as he'd said. She counted the paving slabs: one, two, three, four, five. Then stopped. Her heart pounded in her ears and she breathed slowly to combat the sudden feeling of light-headedness. Number five. She leaned forwards. It looked different from the rest. The rough, broken edges of the others were not visible on this slab. Instead, it had a more rounded appearance, almost like a piece of glass which had been worn by the ocean. It was a slightly different colour too: the rest were grey, whilst this was a terracotta colour. She leaned closer and could feel the drumming in her chest. Closing her eyes briefly, she reached forward and took hold of the slab in both hands. It was much heavier than she had anticipated, and she heaved backwards, groaning under the weight. The earth beneath the stone gave a little and she was able to half-wiggle the slab free of its position. She peered beneath it. Nothing. Her eyes widened and her mouth gaped. Nothing. The hole was there. A perfect box shape. But the box was gone. And then she noticed them . . . the finger marks in the earth, to the top and bottom of where the stone had sat, and she knew that they were not her finger marks and that it was too late. It was then that she got the overwhelming feeling that someone was watching her.

Taking it further

The more the children become used to this approach, the more experimental they will be; eventually the process will become much more organic.

Mise-en-scène

"When people ask me if I went to film school I tell them, 'No, I went to films'." – Quentin Tarantino

'Mise-en-scène' is a term used by film makers to describe the placement of everything we see in the scene. Aspects, such as the use of space, the lighting, the placement of objects in the scene, the costume and the composition, are all carefully planned.

Teaching tip

Freeze the screen and use sticky notes to describe what the children see.

Each of the aspects adds to the overall effect of the scene, and communicates meaning to the watching audience. By transferring some of these techniques into writing, the young writers can create detailed descriptions which allow readers to draw out information about characters and their settings.

In the short animation *Loteria de Navidad*, found on www.literacyshed.com, we follow a lonely security guard called Justino. His apartment is sparsely furnished; a single bed reveals to us that he probably lives alone. A pile of books topped off with a globe suggests that Justino would love to travel, but only reads about it – a suggestion backed up by the maps that cover the walls of his bedroom.

Children writing a setting description could include features in this way in order to meticulously plan what is included for the reader. Ask the children to think like a director – think about composition of the scene, settings – including sound and lighting (this might also include weather), the props, the actors/characters, costume and also what we don't see. It is often a clever authorial 'trick' to note what isn't in the scene:

The bench had room for six, and yet Billy had elected to sit over by the swings, by himself.

One million* questions

"There is frequently more to be learned from the unexpected questions of a child than the discourses of men." – John Locke

More often than not, when children are responding to a picture stimulus in order to write about it, they are responding to questions posed by the teacher. Children and teachers can often interpret images differently, and therefore pose different questions. It is with this in mind that we should sometimes allow the children to create the questions.

Asking the children to create a million* questions about an image or a short section of film will throw up some surprises. Begin by modelling some questions about an image using the key questioning words:

- Who?
- What?
- Why?
- Where?
- When?
- How?

As well as asking the obvious questions, you may ask some more obscure questions about minute details and demonstrate that you can ask questions without knowing what the answer is, e.g. *Why is the house painted blue?* This is probably impossible to answer just by looking at the image. However, it could lead to an imaginative response later.

Children should then ask as many questions about the image using these question words, such as: *Who is he? Why is he wearing that? Where is she going? What is she thinking? How did he get in there?* Once the children have exhausted their questioning powers, they could share questions with a partner, answer each other's questions, and see if their responses were similar or not.

Taking it further

The children could use a number of the answers, linked together, to establish the early threads of an original narrative.

*Maybe a not a million, but quite a few.

Reciprocal viewing

"I love being the predictor. It's a bit like being a detective and solving a mystery!"

Rather than the teacher leading the discussion around a film or animation, allow the children to lead it through a reciprocal viewing process. Like reciprocal reading, it encourages children to be actively involved in the whole discussion, rather than just answering questions posed by the teacher.

Reciprocal viewing encourages children to think about their own thought processes and monitor their understanding of the 'narrative' as they view it. It also encourages pupils to ask more questions during the viewing, which will also lead to greater depth of comprehension.

How to put it into practice:

1. Put pupils into groups of four.
2. Designate each member of the group a role:
   - Summariser
   - Questioner
   - Clarifier
   - Predictor.
3. The summariser will pause the film and explain the key ideas in the film up to this point. You may give specific points to pause the film.
4. The questioner then asks a question about the viewed section – question stems may be provided to scaffold this.
5. The clarifier will lead the discussion, answering these questions and recording their thoughts.
6. The predictor then predicts what they think will happen next.

Repeat until the selected section of film has been viewed. You may wish children to keep the same role for the reading session, or switch roles after each 'pause and discuss'.

Rehearsal of reading skills through film

"Cinematography is a writing with images in movement and with sounds" – Robert Bresson

There are very few activities that can be carried out in the English classroom that is as inclusive as watching a film. Except for those children with very specific learning needs, all children can be involved in discussion of the film they have seen on the screen.

Interpreting a text, and participating in a discussion around these interpretations, is vital for children's development of comprehension skills. For some children, carrying out this discussion around an image, or a film, takes away some of the 'barriers to reading' that they have, such as decoding difficulties or a language deficit. Inferring, or predicting, from a film acts as rehearsal for applying these skills to a text. Film makers must make use of visual clues, and children – often due to the dominance of film in the home – become experts at interpreting the clues.

Use the mnemonic VIPERS to remember the key comprehension areas (see Idea 15).

Each of the key areas can be rehearsed using film or image to reinforce the strategies. For more information about Reading VIPERS visit www.literacyshedblog.com.

Examples of questions using VIPERS
How is the character feeling here? (Inference)

What do you think he will do now he has the treasure? What makes you think this? (Prediction)

Can you describe how the relationship between the girl and her father changed? (Explain/ Summarise)

Teaching tip

Ensure all reading staff are asking questions about each of the key comprehension areas by providing them with generic question stems for each area.

The passing of time

"Blackness enveloped the forest. Its dark arms unfurled through the branches. Night had come."

It is very rare for a film to be played out in actual time. There are some notable exceptions, such as the classic western, *High Noon,* and the television series *24*. Usually, time is slowed down or increased, depending on the desired effect. The passing of time can be shown in a variety of ways.

Telling the reader that a shift has happened
Some films will have a series of events with text indicating the jumps in time, such as *Three weeks later; Ten years later*, or even, *Five years earlier*. This is probably the easiest to emulate in writing. The jumps in time can be written as above, or indicated by using a handy piece of punctuation. The dinkus (three asterisks in a line ***) shows a shift in time has occurred. The writer may leave clues to show that time has passed, rather than explicitly telling the reader how much time has passed.

Showing a clock
An alarm clock ringing can show the start of a new day and a close-up of a wall clock can establish the passage of time for the viewer. This can be developed in writing using examples such as, *He watched the seconds tick by and the hands signalled 11pm*, or *The church clock struck 12*.

Light and dark
Light and dark transitions can show the end of a day. *As darkness fell* indicates evening time, as does the *sun dipping below the horizon*, and other similar descriptions.

Changing seasons

In the film *Notting Hill*, William Thacker leaves his home and begins to walk. The world around him changes to show the passing of time through the seasons: snow, sunshine, wind and rain. This can be used in story writing to show a longer period of time passing, e.g. *The Princess slept. Outside the castle, the blue skies turned to grey, leaves fell from the trees, snow covered the ground, and when spring came, it melted. The bluebells and crocuses unfurled their heads in the warming air, and still she slept.*

The montage

Some films, such as the opening scene from Pixar's *Up*, use a montage to show time passing. This is tricky to emulate in writing, but not impossible. One example could be, *He grew older sitting at the piano. Playing melodic tunes, first for his lover, and then his wife. Then he played with the children by his side begging him to play the happy songs they loved to sing along to, and, one by one, they left until it was just the two of them again. And now . . . now he plays by himself, a mournful refrain at a lonely piano.*

The aging of a character

It is often apparent that time has passed when we see a character age. In *The Lion King*, Simba starts as a cub, but changes into an adult lion. In *Moana*, the main character starts as a child, but changes to an adult. Within writing, this is also possible. This is an easier task when writing in the first person. The aging of the character is usually synchronised with the starting of a new paragraph, as moving from one age to the next is difficult, though not impossible, in one sentence: *She lay in her mother's arms, looking up with big blue eyes: the same big blue eyes which now stood staring at the notice board, searching for her results.*

Taking it further

When watching films with the children, ask them to record as many different ways as they can of the passing of time being shown.

Replacing the soundtrack

"It was exciting knowing that I was going to be on the internet and my mum and dad would be able to watch it."

There is a number of ways of publishing ideas, other than just writing them down in English books. As teachers, we should be providing children with a range of opportunities to publish their work to a wider audience. One way of doing this is to replace the soundtrack of a film, animation, advert or televised speech with the child's own words.

Choose a suitable short section of film for children to produce a spoken response to. It could be a short animation, such as *The Piano*, where pupils record their narrative over the top of the moving image. It could be dialogue between two characters, a narrative poem, or perhaps a description of the setting. It could also be a TV charity appeal, such as those for www.wateraid.org or www.redcross.org.uk, or a persuasive piece of advertising.

The original soundtracks can be analysed for features which could then be included in the children's versions. Children can listen back to their own recordings and redraft them accordingly. Some may want to ensure the images match up with what they are saying.

Adobe Spark Video allows children to insert multiple video clips and images into a project to record a voice-over.

Show, don't tell – action and setting

"One of the cardinal rules of good fiction is never tell us a thing if you can show us." – Stephen King

It is not only the description of characters' feelings and emotions that benefit from the 'show, don't tell' technique, but also setting descriptions or action.

Some films, like *Star Wars*, start by exposing the reader to some text which tells them when and where the film is set. Other films show us a range of sights and sounds which firmly cement the location and time in the viewer's mind. Martin Scorsese, in his film, *Hugo*, leaves us in no doubt that we are watching the action in 1930s Paris. The audience sees the Paris sky, steam trains and passengers in period dress, all whilst listening to a French accordion player sitting outside a small patisserie. The audience cannot help but feel they are on the platform at the Gare du Nord in the 1930s.

We are not imagining that all pupils will turn into Scorsese overnight, but we can help them to take steps on their way.

Tell: It was a cold day in winter.
Show: The boy pulled on his hat and gloves before stepping onto the crisp white grass. His breath misted in front of his face as he crunched through the dead leaves which covered the ground.

Tell: The cat died.
Show: It lay still; its eyes were closed. With a sigh, its chest ceased moving and it looked peaceful, like it was sleeping.

> **Teaching tip**
>
> Find examples in narrative and film to reinforce 'show, don't tell'. Use guided reading time to highlight examples in texts.

Show, don't tell – characters' feelings

"Don't tell me the moon is shining; show me the glint of light on broken glass." – Anton Chekhov

It is a rare thing in a film for a character to tell the audience how they are feeling. There are a number of ways in which the audience can deduce or infer how the character is feeling, and emulating these techniques in writing can enhance a child's composition.

Teaching tip

Once explored, have a range of feelings displayed on the wall that children can access during independent writing.

Even young children, usually due to their prevalent home literacy (TV and film) can infer, deduce and predict from films quite effortlessly and can verbalise how a character is feeling. It is at this point that we really need to ask children, 'How do you know that?'. 'They just look sad!' is a response that often greets me when I ask these questions. 'You can just tell!' others join in. At this point, I ask them to explain what the character did which told them that they were sad. Maybe they are crying, looking at the ground or have their arms folded across their chest, for example. To support this discussion and exploration, ask the children to demonstrate what being sad looks like. Ask their friends to describe their actions and facial expressions. Repeat with a range of expressions in order for the children to experience the actions and expressions. Record their ideas using the headings 'Looks like' and 'Feels like':

> *Nervous*
> *Looks like – wide eyed, grimacing, knees knocking, looking around, pale.*
> *Feels like – butterflies, sweating, goosebumps, hot or cold, can't move.*

This scaffold enables pupils to effectively construct 'show, don't tell' passages of writing.

Meet the experts

"An expert knows all the right answers — if you ask the right questions." — Lévi Strauss

Have you ever sat through a boring training session and felt that what you have learned was of little use? If you could create the perfect professional development session, then what would you want to find out?

The internet is full of experts with answers to your every question. Join in with their excellent ongoing discussions.

8 easy steps for joining online discussions:
1. Join Twitter and choose a username to reflect your passions.
2. Search for topics, keywords or people.
3. Ask questions.
4. Follow English subject hashtags, such as #picbookday or #primaryrocks.
5. Don't be shy — join in conversations.
6. Tweet your experiences in the classroom, both good and bad.
7. Answer questions posed by others.
8. Share examples of work that children in your class or school have completed.

Some interesting people to follow on Twitter:
@primaryrocks1 managed by the Primary Rocks team, but more often than not by @gazneedle

@smithsmm — a primary head who is mad about children's books

@mat_at_brookes — senior lecturer in English and children's literature

@moses_brian — performance poet, percussionist and writer

@ATaleUnfolds — a primary teacher inspiring literacy change through digital media

@shinpad1 — primary deputy and EdD student

Teaching tip

Be mindful before sharing writing by or photographs of children. Ensure you follow your school social media policy.

@MrBoothY6 – another ambassador for
  children's literature
@Patronofreading – working with UK schools
  to develop author relationships.

Visit this blog to find even more wonderful
people to follow:

www.literacyshedblog.com/blog/another-50-
primary-focussed-tweeters-you-probably-
should-be-following

Taking it further

Here are just a few great
authors to follow:

@moontrug – Abi
Elphinstone

@RossAuthor – Ross
MacKenzie

@whatSFSaid – SFSaid.